WHAT'S IN STYLE
FIREPLACES

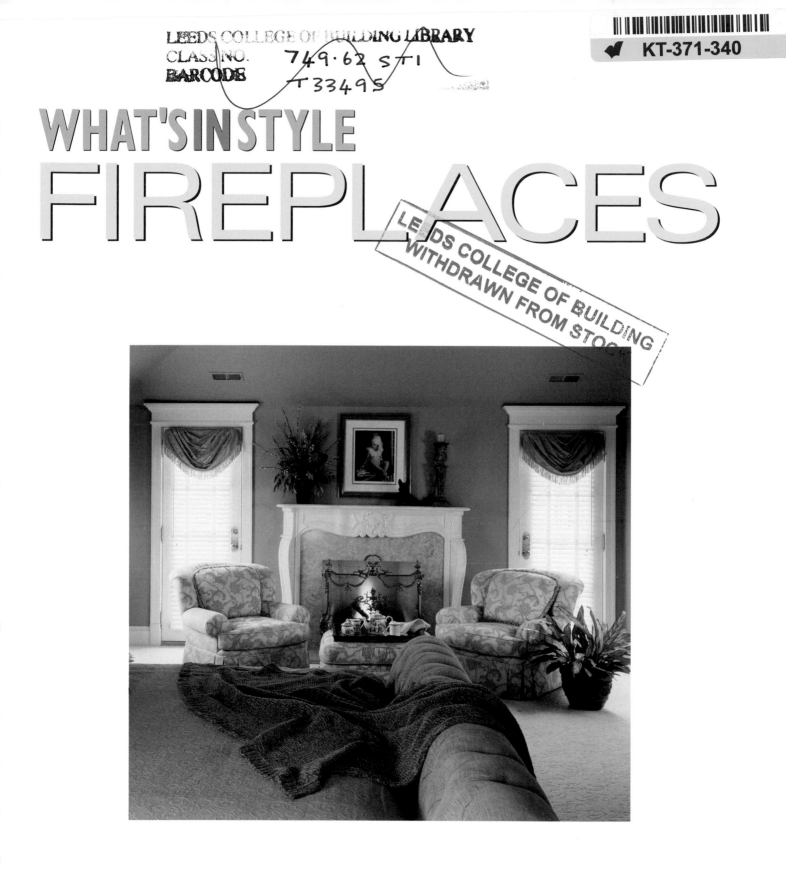

WHAT'S IN STYLE
FIREPLACES

Joanne Still

CREATIVE HOMEOWNER®, Upper Saddle River, New Jersey

Editorial Director: Timothy O. Bakke
Production Manager: Kimberly H. Vivas

Senior Editor, Home Decorating: Kathie Robitz
Editor, Home Decorating: Therese Hoehlein Cerbie
Assistant Editor and Photo Researcher: Sharon Ranftle
Copy Editor: Bruce Wetterau
Editorial Assistant: Jennifer Ramcke
Indexer: Schroeder Indexing Services

Book Designer: Stephanie Phelan
Graphic Designer: Scott Molenaro
Cover Design: Scott Molenaro
Front Cover Photography: Beth Singer
Back Cover Photography: (top left) Jessie Walker, (top right) Beth Singer, (bottom) Mark Samu

Advice for curing a clay chiminea, which appears on page 75, provided by Russ Turina.

Manufactured in the United States of America

Current Printing (last digit)
10 9 8 7 6

What's in Style—Fireplaces, First Edition
Library of Congress Control Number: 2002104991
ISBN: 1-58011-116-5

CREATIVE HOMEOWNER®
A Division of Federal Marketing Corp.
24 Park Way, Upper Saddle River, NJ 07458
www.creativehomeowner.com

acknowledgments

Fire is an ancient gift, the blessings and need for which humanity has never outgrown. It is no accident that we use the word "warm" to describe people and places that provide us with feelings of comfort and safety, often as a result of help generously and willingly given. My warmest thanks to Michael O'Connor of the Mad Hatter Chimney Sweep Company, Stone Ridge, New York; Ashley Eldridge of the Chimney Safety Institute of America and the National Chimney Sweep Guild; and Kathie Robitz, a uniquely gifted editor, facilitator, and maker of beautiful things.

contents

introduction

Let the warmth of a fireplace **increase your comfort** and the **value of your house** with style and up-to-the-minute efficient, environmentally **responsible designs.**

What is it about the golden glow that fills a room from a fireplace or woodstove? What draws us to the flames of the outdoor fireplace, fire pit, or chiminea? It's so much more than decorative ambiance or even the practicality of an alternative heat source. *What's In Style—Fireplaces* offers an explanation, beginning with Chapter 1, "The Lure of the Fire, " which offers some of the highlights of humanity's millennia-old connection to fire, from the powerful blaze of prehistoric peoples to the dancing flames of our modern adaptations of that primitive necessity. It may put into perspective something of the alluring power of a fire, and inspire plans of your own.

In addition to inspiration, *What's in Style—Fireplaces* provides useful information. Consult Chapter 2, "Blazing a Style," for an overview of fireplaces, including specific architectural forms and period details (Baroque, Federal, Arts and Crafts, for example) plus today's classics: traditional, country, and contemporary styles. Also in this chapter you'll read how the right furnishings and accessories can help create a cohesive style in a room containing a fireplace. And if an updated appearance is what your fireplace needs, there are lots of ideas for changing the fireplace mantel or surround.

Looking for advice about how to design a room and furnish it to take the best advantage of the warmth and atmosphere a fireplace offers? Chapter 3, "Fireside Arrangements," can help with easy suggestions that make a fireplace the focal point of a room, show you how to arrange everything to take advantage of the heat, and help you work around or downplay an odd-size fireplace or one that's in an awkward location. What about art or other decorative displays around the fireplace or on the mantel? If you've ever been perplexed about creating an interesting, comfortable arrangement of furniture and accessories, then here's what you need to know. Plus, you'll find suggestions for mantel displays and wall art, too.

Advances in technology over the past few decades have provided alternatives to wood as a fuel option. Gas fireplaces and stoves—the fastest-growing segment of the marketplace—have become the most popular choice, especially as the industry has improved heat output and created more-realistic-looking logs and flames. And there are convenient extras to consider, such as remote-control ignition and adjustment of the blaze. Chapter 4, "Today's Technology," examines these options, along with advice for maintaining a healthy fireplace environment.

Step outside for a moment and imagine the coziness of a fire in your yard or on your deck or patio. It's easy to create a "living room" feeling in the great outdoors with a built-in fireplace or fire pit or a movable appliance such as a manufactured fireplace or a Mexican stack oven (known as a chiminea). *What's in Style—Fireplaces* presents numerous possibilities in Chapter 5, "Outdoor Fire." There are so many great product choices today, including portable as well as freestanding

and built-in models. And if you're just looking for a little heat to keep your outdoor dining area comfortable on cool evenings, consider one of the attractive "outdoor heaters," which fit on any patio, porch, or deck. Some of them can stand on your tabletop—a perfect solution for a small balcony or outdoor area.

Is a wood, gas, or pellet stove a better choice for you than a fireplace? Think about it as you read Chapter 6, "The Latest Stoves," which presents an array of the twenty-first century's safest and best-looking wood,

gas, or pellet stoves on the market. Included is an explanation of features that make today's stoves efficient and environmentally friendly appliances.

Chapter 7, "Tools and Accessories," provides a cavalcade of the implements and additional items that can enhance your hearthside enjoyment. In addition to the practical firemaking and maintenance basics such as andirons, grates, bellows, pokers, tongs, shovels, and brushes, manufacturers and artisans offer a collection of other related items that make the most of the hearth of the home.

Finally, the Resources at the back of the book provide a handy service when you're ready to shop. Check out the manufacturers in the listing as well as the professional associations, which offer additional insight into design and installation matters.

So if you're thinking about updating an old fireplace, installing a new one, or even adding a second unit, but you're hesitating about the cost, keep this in mind: today's devices will increase the value of your house when you decide to sell. In most cases, owning a fireplace is a smart investment.

1
the lure
of the fire

Home and hearth have always gone together, and remain **synonymous** with **comfort** even today.

Few things in the modern world connect people so directly to their primitive origins as does a fire in the hearth. Anthropologists report that the earliest uses for fire—beginning more than a million years ago—were for cooking and warmth, so it's easy to imagine how people would still be drawn to fire as a symbol of survival, comfort, and community. Because the earliest humans were nomadic hunters of game and gatherers of edible and medicinal plants, fire probably blazed outdoors. Later, as agriculture developed, so did the concept of permanent dwellings. At the same time, primitive people discovered that fire could be moved into a sheltered area if there was a hole in the ceiling of the cave or dwelling to allow heated smoky air to rise and escape while cool air entered through openings near the floor. The next innovation was the stacking of materials around the hole in the ceiling, which drew the heated smoke upward more effectively. Thus, the primitive chimney was created.

Although the Romans probably did not have fireplaces per se, they did build a system of ducts under the floors of public buildings and baths. These ducts began above the fires that were maintained beneath the buildings, and the warm air traveled up through the ducts to the buildings. Credit for the invention of the fireplace itself, however, goes to the Norman invaders of England, who needed a method of heating their immense, multiple-story stone castles. The Normans created a system in which one chimney served the fireplaces on several different stories. The medieval poor, meanwhile, who could not afford the

materials nor spare the time it would take to construct fireplaces, continued to use the open hearth. In fact, the open hearth, which was extremely serviceable albeit modest in scope, continued to exist in dwellings constructed through the seventeenth century.

EARLY DECORATED FIREPLACES

With the relative political stability that gradually emerged in Europe starting in the fourteenth century came the aesthetic and stylistic changes in all areas of life and a period called the Renaissance. By about the sixteenth century, these changes were reflected in the aesthetics of a fireplace. Ornate adornment became commonplace. As time passed, fireplace design continued to mirror changing tastes. In 1796, the first Rumford fireplace appeared in America. With a tall streamlined throat at the base of the chimney, it was not only more efficient but elegant and fine looking.

In the late nineteenth and early twentieth centuries, more-efficient methods—steam, then oil, and later, electricity—were developed for producing heat and cooking food. These new methods, and the related devices and appliances that were invented as a result, caused a gradual phasing out of the fireplace's previous functions and of the fireplace itself.

Once the fireplace lost its utilitarian value, it became appreciated for its aesthetics. No longer considered a necessity, it became a luxury and, consequently, a symbol of status and wealth. Expensive finishing materials, such as marble, and handcrafted details such as painted tiles, gilding, carving, and relief motifs added sophistication. So by the middle of the twentieth century, the fireplace had become an extraneous but desirable artifact.

Although people have not needed the fireplace for

Handsome details, such as painted tiles on the face of a fireplace, above, or ornate carved stone, opposite, would have been strictly for the wealthy at one time.

cooking or as a source of home heating for about a century, many new and restored homes include at least one fireplace in their plans. Why? Perhaps the persistent popularity of fireplaces and their near relatives lay in echoes of the lives of our distant ancestors: the hunter on the plains who survived the night because fire kept predators from the camp; the medieval family who gathered around the hearth to feast and celebrate the workday's end; the pride symbolized by the mantel and overmantel displays of heirlooms or crests that told of a family's achievements and the ideals it lived by. The lure of the fire has a romantic history and, no doubt, a future that will last as long as humans gather together.

The Modern Fireplace

Even today, a fireplace lends a bit of modern romance and warmth to a home. In general, there are three types of fireplaces: masonry, the traditional choice, which is constructed only of bricks and mortar; manufactured, consisting of a metal firebox and metal chimney; and

A Quick Guide to Buying Firewood

How much wood you need to buy in a season depends on a number of factors, but there are three major variables: how often and how long you burn fires; the efficiency of your fireplace or stove; and the type of wood you burn. In general, hard, dense woods are ideal for fuel. As a rule of thumb, the wood from deciduous trees is best. (Deciduous trees are those that shed their leaves annually.) These include oak, maple, walnut, birch, beech, ash, and the wood from fruit trees such as cherry and apple.

Avoid burning wood from evergreens—those cone-bearing (coniferous) trees with needles instead of leaves. The wood of coniferous trees is soft and it will burn faster, so a greater volume of wood will be consumed per hour compared with hardwood. A greater problem with softwoods, however, is the resin content. Resin is the gummy substance that's used in the manufacture of some wood stains and shellacs, and when resin is burned it gives off a byproduct called creosote. Creosote, which is flammable, accumulates in flues and chimneys, and this buildup represents a potential fire hazard.

The wood you purchase should also be seasoned, which means that the tree should have been cut down at least six months or, preferably, a year prior to the burning of the wood. Ideally, the wood should be cut and split soon after the tree is felled, allowing for more effective drying. The moisture in unseasoned (or green) wood tends to have a cooling effect, preventing complete combustion and making it harder to keep a fire blazing. A low-burning fire also increases creosote. (It's okay to burn green wood occasionally, but make sure to use small logs or split sticks and add them to an already hot fire.) Conversely, the dryer the logs, the hotter the fire, the less attention the fire needs, and the slower the process of creosote buildup.

hybrid, a type that combines both masonry and metal elements (most commonly, a metal firebox and smoke chamber with a brick chimney).

Regardless of the type, the basic working parts are the same in all modern fireplaces. However, there are some features that are either optional or simply related to the kind of fireplace that you own. The most common parts are discussed here.

Ash dump. Some fireplaces have an enclosed system, called

Traditional architectural forms and masonry construction are still popular today, as exemplified by the older fireplace, below, and the new one, opposite.

the ash dump, for conveniently clearing ash from the hearth so that you don't have to carry it through the living areas. A door at the back of the firebox covers a passageway to a chamber or ash pit below (usually the basement). When the ashes are cold you can sweep them into the pit where they can remain until you remove them.

Chimney. The chimney, which is sometimes called "the stack," is the part of the system that carries smoke and other byproducts of the burning fire (such as hot air, gases, and minute, unburned particles) upward, through the roof of your house, and out into the atmosphere. A chimney may be made of various materials, including

brick, clay, concrete, and insulated stainless steel. The interior passageway of a masonry chimney is usually lined with clay.

Damper. The damper, which often resembles a plate, is actually a movable device that spans the lower end of the smoke chamber to open or close the flue. All wood-burning, and some gas-powered, fireplaces require a damper.

Firebox. The firebox holds the burning fuel and fire. Sometimes it's called the fire chamber.

Flue. A passageway called the flue carries the byproducts of burning fuel—heat, smoke, gases, and unburned particles—to the outside air. A chimney flue is the shaft within a chimney.

Hearth. Technically, the hearth is the term that refers the floor of the firebox, although many people refer to the fireplace itself as "the hearth." Maybe that's because

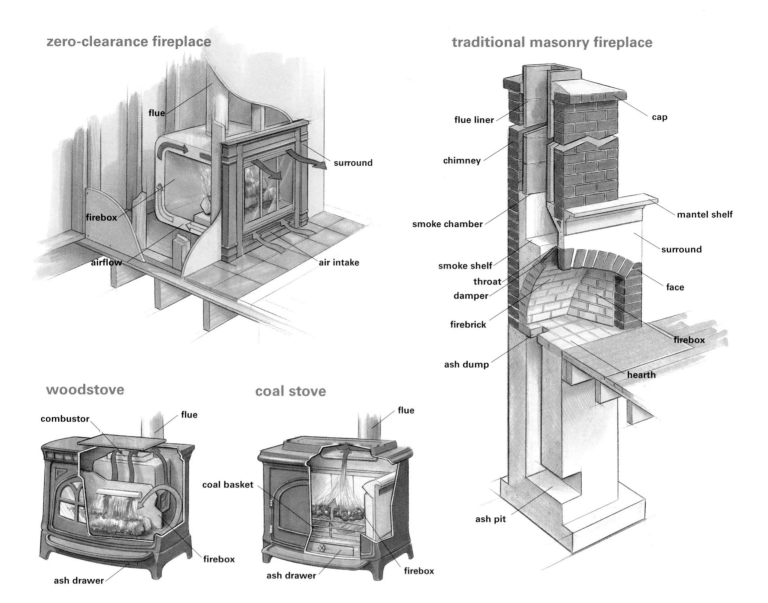

zero-clearance fireplace

flue

surround

firebox

airflow

air intake

traditional masonry fireplace

flue liner

cap

chimney

smoke chamber

mantel shelf

surround

smoke shelf

throat

damper

face

firebrick

firebox

ash dump

hearth

ash pit

woodstove

combustor

flue

firebox

ash drawer

coal stove

flue

coal basket

firebox

ash drawer

the hearth can extend beyond the firebox and into the room just in front of the fireplace.

Lintel. The lintel is a horizontal support that spans the top opening at the front of the firebox.

Smoke chamber. This is the area between the damper and the beginning of the flue.

Throat. A narrow opening located over the firebox,

the throat aids the flow of smoke, gases, and flames into the smoke chamber, and eventually out through the chimney.

Smoke shelf. The floor at the back of the smoke chamber is called the smoke shelf.

"Surround" is the word that refers to the facing ornamentation mounted at the sides and top of the fireplace opening. A "mantel" is a shelf or other facing ornamentation that is mounted above and across the fireplace. Both the mantel and the surround play a role in establishing not only the architecture of the fireplace but of the house itself. There are many contemporary, traditional, and period styles, as you'll see in the chapters that follow.

Considered obsolete for much of the twentieth century, fireplaces have increased in popularity over the last 20 years. **Warm and welcoming,** the newly constructed fireplace on the opposite page embodies the type of nostalgic appeal that makes a house a home.

a portfolio of stylish design

blazing
a style

A **fireplace** can add **period details** or borrow **elements** from the **architectural** character of a house.

For many people, having a fireplace is about creating ambiance. Because most homeowners simply like the looks and cozy feeling of a fire, it's the aesthetic consideration, not the need for heat, that makes a fireplace a popular amenity in a house today. Typically, the style of a fireplace will be in keeping with the architecture and decor of the house. But there are no rules that say this has to be the case. As with all style issues, personal taste is the ultimate determining factor. As long as the structure of the fireplace conforms to mandated building codes, how you finish it is your choice. Whether you are giving an older fireplace a face-lift or installing a new one, keep in mind that this important architectural feature can be a starting point for pulling together the interior design of the room. You might take this into account if your fireplace is style-specific, such as a Craftsman design with its dark oak beams and earth-tone tiles, or a kiva, the unique adobe corner fireplace of the Southwest. Otherwise, its "style" may fall into a category that is not as easily defined except in general terms such as traditional, rustic, or contemporary. A finished look might even incorporate elements from various architectural styles. In this chapter, you'll get to know the characteristics of many designs, which range from casual and eclectic to formal or strictly period. Look for features that you think complement the style of your house, or go in a completely new direction. You can even make your fireplace look as if it was transported from a fifteenth-century French chateau, if that's to your liking. With so many materials and the technology that's available today, your choices are almost unlimited.

Designer Tip

Period designs may be costly to re-create, but you can be true to the essence of a style without copying it exactly. Add period details in prefabricated moldings and composition ornament. Pull the look together with mantel accessories, color, and wall art that mirror the style as well.

STYLE TRENDS

Currently, builders often combine various elements of different styles and periods into new houses, and fireplaces tend toward a similar eclecticism. For example, classical features such as columns or corbels are incorporated into otherwise contemporary fireplaces. With the prevalence of vaulted ceilings, some fireplaces have also become proportionately grand in scale and equally dramatic in decoration. As for finishing materials, many of them—wood, brick, ceramic tile, river rock, and marble—are simply classic. Granite and limestone are particularly popular choices, especially if you want a sleek contemporary design. Other good-looking contemporary materials include reinforced concrete and cast stone, which are less load bearing but more affordable than granite and cut limestone, and can

New meets Old World, above, with Baroque-inspired columns. Paint spruces up a 1950s brick facade, right. Ornamental elements distinguish the fireplace opposite.

be used to affordably reproduce handsome Old World designs or give the look of natural stone.

If you are debating about the finished look you want for a new fireplace or considering refinishing the mantel or facade of an old model, it may help to study some of the established decorative styles that present-day architects and craftspeople are using as inspiration.

Evolution of European Designs

Although the earliest decorative fireplace surrounds in Europe probably date to the twelfth century, it wasn't until a couple of centuries later, when hoods and canopies to channel smoke up the chimney came into use, that a real style started to emerge. In Tudor and Elizabethan England, arched facings were typical. Later, elaborate corbels, carvings, and coats of arms crafted in stone and wood decorated those canopies and hoods. Even the overmantel was adorned with over-the-top combinations of motifs, typically virgins, crests, mottoes, family trees, scrolls, medallions, and initials, among other ornamentation.

In southern Europe, stone or adobe fireplaces prevailed, especially in rustic regions. As for the opulent homes of the wealthy, flamboyant tiles might bedeck the entire interior of a fireplace decoration in Spain, while in Italy carved stone and marble and tiled surrounds were the chosen decorative elements. During the early Renaissance, classical details borrowed from Roman and Greek antiquity began to appear on fireplace mantels, and craftsmen continually refined these details into the High Renaissance era. In the peasant homes of northern France, raw mortared stone and heavy oak lintels contrasted with the sculpted marble or stone mantels and majolica surrounds of grand homes.

A contemporary version of an adobe fireplace, left, reinforces the Southwest vernacular in the architecture here. European tile adds an authentic air to a Spanish mission style, right, while gingerbread enhances a whimsical take on Victoriana, top right.

Baroque and Rococo. In reaction to the classicism of the High Renaissance period of the fifteenth and sixteenth centuries, seventeenth-century Europe (particularly France, Germany, and Italy) moved toward an exaggerated, rich, and often excessive form of decoration called Baroque. Marble, imitation stone, ornate gilt, and fantastic ornament decorated the furnishings and fireplaces of the period. Oversize swirling columns and other exaggerated motifs characterize this masculine, over-the-top style. In the eighteenth century, Baroque was followed by Rococo, a softer, prettier version of the style. Typical carved fireplace motifs of the Rococo period might include flora and fauna; leaves and flowers intermingled with shells and rocks; or pretty curls and curvaceous abstract shapes.

Georgian and Regency. In England, design took a more restrained turn over the course of the eighteenth and early nineteenth centuries. Spurred by the excavations of Pompeii and other finds of antiquity, architects and furniture designers moved away from the excesses of Rococo and into a new age of classicism, elegance, and symmetry. Once again designers borrowed from the Greeks and Romans, using such motifs as columns, urns, capitals, acanthus leaves, fluted pilasters, and moldings to create elegant mantels, overmantels, and surrounds. Sometimes they included designs in bas relief in stucco or marble. Robert Adam and other English architects of the Georgian period contrived intricate inlays of different color marbles. Even the wood paneling around the fireplace might be tinted a pastel to match the natural materials used on the fireplace itself. Pure geometry

Stone and wood captures timeless drama, above. **The look of carved stone,** opposite bottom, brings European-style sophistication to a room, while **antiqued wood and tin,** opposite top, appears surprisingly fresh.

Experiment with faux effects to add an aged look or a specific style to a fireplace mantel and surround. Craft stores sell inexpensive kits with directions for adding the appearance of antiqued or paneled wood or plaster, rusticated stone, marble, terra cotta, and other effects that make any style achievable.

defined the English Regency style of the early nineteenth century. Although they are classical, Regency forms are also rectilinear and spare.

Style Comes to America

The very earliest American fireplaces, those of the seventeenth century, were cozy and plain. With a surround made of stone, the fireplace mantel typically consisted of a lintel and a shelf that held cooking utensils and plates. As the towns and cities evolved, however, American tastes changed. By the 1700s, people in the New World began to desire some of the sophistication of Europe. The fireplace designs in prosperous American homes emulated those of Georgian England, even after the war for independence had been won.

Federal. This period began with the American Revolution and continued into the early years of the Republic. In many ways it is Georgian with references to classicism and

symmetrical lines. There are also elements of French influence, particularly in symbols of the French Revolution—stars, for example—or patriotism as well as simplicity and grace. A surround of fine carved wood, often mahogany, was typical. The Federal style remained popular until the second half of the nineteenth century.

Victorian. Both in the United States and England, the Industrial Revolution during the second half of the 1800s ushered in the Victorian era and a trend toward flamboyance. Elaborate mantels displayed all kinds of

trinkets, and the overmantel was elaborately carved. The Victorians loved to mix and match ornament. Ornamental details might be borrowed from many periods, styles, and parts of the world. Moorish and Oriental influences are prevalent in many designs. Dark woods and marbles and pictorial tiles also became fashionable.

A Modern Aesthetic

By the late 1800s, the Victorian excesses in decoration and the near-elimination of the artisan through mass production caused a revolt. New art movements took place. A renewed respect for hand craftsmanship and natural materials grew out of this thinking, and the innovative work of some of the architects and designers of the time significantly influenced twentieth-century design, including the architecture of fireplaces.

A flamboyant mural, left, is wildly stylish, but the simple shelf mantel with dentil molding keeps it grounded.
Rustic river rock becomes refined, above, when it's paired successfully with a graceful painted wooden shelf mantel in this cozy cottage family room.

Arts and Crafts. A movement of the late nineteenth and early twentieth century, Arts and Crafts, or Craftsman, emphasizes organic materials and forms. Simple motifs, a plain surround and mantel fabricated perhaps in brick and oak, and squared off lines are typical of Arts and Crafts designs. Sometimes handmade tile around the hearth was used to add rich, nature-inspired colors to the look.

Art Nouveau. Japanese art and the Arts and Crafts movement inspired this period, which lasted from about 1910 until after the first World War. Motifs that decorated Art Nouveau-style fireplaces included sinuous lines and curves of an organic nature, particularly plant forms. Ceramic tiles in pink, maroon, gray, or green often decorated the surround or mantelpiece.

Art Deco. During the 1920s and 1930s, fireplaces assumed a new palette, from bright colors to soft pastels, thanks to inventive uses of inlays and lacquers. The Art Deco look was different in another way. Its lines were geometric—tubular as well as rectilinear—and its materials urbane: the use of glass or brushed steel on the surround or mantel, for example.

Designer Tip

An excellent finishing material for a fireplace is tile. Luckily, there are reproductions of art tiles today. Most showrooms carry examples of Arts and Crafts, Art Nouveau, California, Delft, and other European tiles. Granite, limestone, and marble tiles are affordable alternatives to custom stone slabs.

MORE HELPFUL IDEAS

Fireplace Face-lift

How can you give an old fireplace a cosmetic update? One place to start is with a thorough cleaning and by patching and repairing any damaged areas. Repointing an old brick surround can certainly give it a lift. Tiling is an excellent way to create an Arts and Crafts look—for example, with reproduction tiles. Add European flair with painted ceramic tiles, drama with a mosaic design, or sleek contemporary styling with granite, terrazzo, or limestone tiles. Painting a wood surround with a faux marble or faux bois (wood) technique is relatively easy and inexpensive.

Add a simple wooden shelf mantel. They come prefabricated in various sizes, and they are ready to stain or paint. This is an easy project that can add lots of architectural character.

Contemporary Style

For much of the twentieth century, fireplaces were out of fashion because they were no longer practical. But today they are popular again, as are all of the styles listed above and then some. It's not unusual to see one or more vintage styles combined in one design. For something to be strictly Contemporary, the lines are clean, ornament is minimal, and fabrication might be in stone (granite or limestone mostly), tile, reinforced concrete, metal, wood, or a combination of these materials.

Fireplaces can underscore an overall look or motif if not an exact style of decoration or architecture. Examples of this are depicted here and include: French chateau, opposite; Contemporary, above; and Art Deco, right.

a portfolio of stylish design

3
fireside arrangements

An **artful placement** of furniture and accessories can add to **the allure** and **appearance** of a fireplace.

Creating an attractive, comfortable setting around a fireplace should be easy. Who doesn't like the cozy ambiance of relaxing in front of a fire? Plus, a fireplace is a natural focal point in a room, an anchor for the overall design, as well as an important architectural feature. But there are times when the presence of a fireplace in a room poses problems with the layout. A fireplace does take up considerable floor and wall space, and like any other permanent feature or built-in piece of furniture, its size or position can limit the possibilities for arranging other furnishings. And what if the size of the fireplace is out of proportion to the space, or what if it's located in an awkward spot? Is there something you can do, short of making structural changes, that will allow you to modify any limitations posed by the position, shape, or scale of the fireplace? As your room is arranged now, are you taking full advantage of your fireplace? Do the accessories on the mantel top, personal collections, and the wall art underscore or undermine its visual appeal? Simple trial and error—experimenting with the existing floor plan or rethinking accessories—may solve these problems, or it may take a studied approach.

In some cases, the fireplace may be just one of several focal points, especially in a large space or an open-plan design. In a living room or family room, it may share the spotlight with an entertainment unit; in a dining room, with a spectacular chandelier; or in a bedroom, with a dramatic four-poster bed. As a standard feature of many new homes, large windows command attention and add visual weight to a room, as do other currently

popular architectural elements, such as stately columns and voluminous vaulted ceilings. Features such as these may compete with a fireplace unless you can find a way to balance them within your scheme. When matters involve multiple considerations, it's best to rely on the universal principles of good design for making a fireplace an enjoyable part of your lifestyle, as well as a showpiece that will invite repeated use.

In a room with a high ceiling, opposite, a large painting creates necessary drama over the fireplace, while **a chandelier** properly fills the space above another mantel, right. **A balanced fireside arrangement**, below, underscores the symmetry of the doors.

THE FIREPLACE AND THE SPACE

What is the room's size and shape—large, small, square, long and narrow, L-shaped? Where is the fireplace located—in the center of a wall, to the side, or in a corner? What other permanent features, such as windows, doors, bookcases, or media units, will you have to work with in your arrangement? If you can empty the room, do it. That's the best way to study the architecture and the space. Otherwise, clear out whatever clutter there is, and use your imagination—along with a measuring tape. Measure everything, permanent and freestanding pieces. How much clearance can you allow around the furniture for easy passage? How close do you want to be to the fire? Take notes. Then slowly bring things back into the room, arranging as you go, and moving things around as necessary.

Look at the objects on the mantel. Do they form a cohesive arrangement? How about art or objects on the walls above and to the sides of the fireplace. Is there a pleasing relationship between them and the fireplace? If they don't look right to you, edit your choices. Perform the same exercise you did with the furniture, removing everything, and then slowly bringing back objects and trying out different vignettes.

Scale and Proportion. Remember the importance of spatial relationships. For example, a fireplace may seem large in a room with a low ceiling; conversely, it may appear

---

On the mantel above, the repetition of white unites disparate ceramic pieces to create an understated yet standout collection. **Grouping numerous small items,** opposite, compensates for their modest scale. **A large sailboat,** opposite top, attached to the tall wall, compensates for a proportionately squat fireplace.

small in a room with a vaulted ceiling. Size is relative. Applied to objects on the mantel or the wall above the fireplace, correct scale and proportion happen when the objects are the appropriate size for the wall or the fireplace, or even for objects that are near to one another.

Balance. Sometimes the architectural features of a mantel or surround are so strong, you'll have to match them with furnishings of equal visual weight. Or they may be so ornate or plain that you'll have to play them up or tone them down to make them work with the rest of the decor. That's balance. But balance also refers to arrangements: symmetrical, asymmetrical, and radial. Examples of each are included later in this chapter.

Line. Shape depends on line. Different types of lines suggest various qualities. Pay attention to the lines when you're creating arrangements and relationships among objects. Some lines are inherent in a room or an architectural feature. But you can modify them. For example: vertical lines are stately and dignified, which is just the look you want for

Designer Tip

Compose groupings of objects of different heights for visual interest—a straight line can be boring. Raise one or two pieces with a small pedestal, book, or stand. Stagger the pieces from back to front. If you have three objects, make a triangle. If there are more, create overlapping triangles.

fireside arrangements **43**

your fireplace, but unfortunately, it's rather wide and squat instead. Solution? Create an arrangement above the fireplace that extends high on the wall, or hang a tall mirror or frame over than mantel. For reinforcement, place tall-back chairs or torchères on either side of the fireplace.

What if the fireplace is too tall? Does it overwhelm the rest of the furniture? Add horizontal lines by moving seating pieces farther apart to the right and left of the hearth. Install wall art on the sides of the fireplace, but be careful not to hang it too high on the wall.

If the room is boxy, avoid grouping pieces at right angles to the fireplace and each other. Instead, de-

---

Modular seating pieces permit a flexible floor plan in a small family room, opposite. **Placing furniture in the center** of a large space in front of the hearth, above, adds to the intimacy and coziness of this living room.

emphasize the boxy shape by placing them on the diagonal to open the square. Use upholstered pieces with rounded arms or curvaceous cushions, legs, or frames. Create a radial arrangement. With the hearth as the central point, create a semicircular hub of furnishings that include seating and a small table or two.

Don't forget that too many straight lines are boring and rigid. Find a way to soften them with a round area rug, an oval table or mirror, or even an arrangement of wall objects hung in a circle above the mantel.

Rhythm. Keep the eye moving at a measured pace by repeating motifs, colors, or shapes. For example, you might pick up the color from a tiled surround to use as an accent color in fabrics on upholstered pieces, curtains, pillows and throws, or other decorative accessories. Or repeat architectural features of the fireplace with other similar elements in the room, such as molding or other woodwork details.

Variety. Don't go overboard trying to match everything exactly. The most interesting rooms and arrangements mix objects of different sizes, shapes, lines, and sometimes even styles (as long as they are compatible). When you're putting together art for the wall above the fireplace or gathering objects for the mantel, this is an opportunity for creating variety. If you're afraid to experiment because you think the result will be disjointed, consider the next design principle.

Harmony. Create harmony among all of the parts of your design by connecting all of the elements either by color or motif. You might have a display of family photos on your mantel. The frames may all be different shapes, styles, and heights, but because each one is made of brass, the overall appearance of the grouping looks harmonious. Or you could assemble a wall vignette of frames over the fireplace, all different in finish but tied together by the subject matter of each one—all landscapes, for example, or all pink cabbage roses. Unifying diverse items in this way creates a finished scheme that is exciting and comfortable at the same time.

Symmetrical versus Asymmetrical Arrangements

If you like the symmetry of classic design, balance your arranged pieces accordingly. For example, position two sofas or love seats of the same size perpendicular to the fireplace and exactly opposite each other. Or place a single sofa parallel with the fireplace, with two chairs opposite one another and equidistant from both the sofa and the hearth. Try out a low coffee table or an oversize ottoman in the center of the arrangement. Leave the peripheral areas outside the main grouping for creating small impromptu conversation areas during parties and gatherings or to accommodate a modest dining area or home-office station.

Asymmetry, applied to the mantel scape above left, looks clean and contemporary, while it makes the period display, left, appear less stuffy. **Symmetry,** on the other hand, aptly serves a formal interior, opposite.

If your design sense is less formal or contemporary, try an asymmetrical grouping in front of the fire. Turn seating pieces at a 45-degree angle from the hearth. In a large open space, locate seating not directly in front of the hearth but slightly off to the side. Counterbalance the arrangement with a large table and chairs, a hutch, bookcases, or any element of relatively equal weight. This layout works especially well when the ceiling is vaulted (as most great rooms are) or when the hearth is massive. In many contemporary homes, especially where there is a zero-clearance unit, the fireplace is not on an outside wall, nor is it necessarily in a central location. (See Chapter 4, "Today's Technology," beginning on page 56, for more information on zero-clearance fireplaces.) This means you can put the fireplace almost anywhere.

COMFORTABLE ARRANGEMENTS

You say you want an intimate environment in front of the fire, but the room is so large it feels and looks impersonal. Large rooms afford lots of leeway for arranging, but people often make the mistake of pushing all of the furniture against the walls. If that's what you're doing, pull the major seating pieces closer together and

Versatile seating around a fire might include large ottomans like the ones paired with the sofas above. **Angling the TV** in the room on the opposite page, top, lets the homeowner enjoy a fire as well as a show. **A picture light** draws attention to artwork without taking away from the appeal of the hearth, opposite bottom.

near the fire, keeping a distance of only 4 to 10 feet between sofas and chairs. For the most comfortable result, create one or more small groupings that can accommodate up to four to six people in different areas of the room.

Instead of a standard sofa and chairs, consider the convenience of modular seating, too, which comes in any number of armless and single-arm end pieces. The advantage of these separate upholstered units is that you can easily add, take away, or rearrange the modules to suit any of your layout or seating needs. Create an L or a U arrangement in front of the fire; subtract pieces, moving one or two outside of the area for an intimate grouping. Use an area rug to further define the space. Or put the pieces together to make one large arrangement in any configuration. Versatile furnishings such as an

ottoman with a hinged top or an antique trunk can double as seating, a low table, or storage.

Small Space Solutions

There are no rules, but for safety and comfort, experts recommend 3-foot-wide aisles for moving from one area of a room to another. If you can't afford that much space,

Mantel-top and over-the-mantel displays bring personality to a room. **A painting** adds a touch of the English countryside, left, while **an old clock face and decoys**, right, add rustic charm to a Colonial cabin. **A mirror and a collection of silver objects** lend sparkle and grace to a casual, sunny seaside cottage.

COMPETING INTERESTS

What should you do if the only place for the television is next to the fireplace? If the TV is small enough to keep on a cart that you can wheel away when the set is not in use, that's ideal. But with cable hookups, VCRs, DVDs, and large-screen TVs, that might be impractical. A cabinet that lets you store the all of this equipment behind closed doors may be the answer, especially if the storage unit is part of a large built-in paneled wall system that incorporates the fireplace into its overall design.

When large windows or glass doors share the wall with a fireplace, easy-to-adjust window treatments are essential: drapery panels on a traverse rod or suspended from rings on a pole, or shutters, shades, or blinds are options. By all means, let the sun shine in during the day. But a pleasant window view by day just becomes a large dark hole at night. So in the evening, close the curtains while the fire sets the mood, whether you're entertaining or relaxing alone.

do the best you can. Select small-scale furnishings: a love seat rather than a sofa, for example, and portable chairs and tables, especially ones with casters that allow you to move them out of the way easily and against the walls when you have a crowd. You can add casters to pieces you already own, too. If you need legs shortened a bit, a carpenter can do that for you inexpensively.

When it's possible, try to leave about 4 feet of space between a coffee table and a sofa so that you can spread your legs out when you're seated. Make use of the largest upholstered ottoman you can squeeze in. It can double as extra seating, a coffee table, or an extension of an easy chair or love seat that lets you put your legs up to relax. Or just keep furniture to a minimum of what you require normally. You can always rely on folding chairs and tables that store flat in a closet or even under the bed when they're not needed.

Avoid area rugs, which can visually divide up a small room into even smaller sections. Stick to one flooring material throughout the space: a light wood floor or room-size rug or a wall-to wall carpet. Avoid a busy or complex design. Keep fabrics and walls simple and light, too. This will make the room appear less crowded.

Mantel Vignettes

A grouping of objects on your mantel can be as simple or complex as you like. To make your display lively, choose a variety of shapes and sizes. For dramatic impact, group related objects that you can link in theme or color. Refer back to the concepts of scale and proportion, balance, line, rhythm, and harmony.

Remember that a symmetrical arrangement has classical overtones and will reinforce the formality of traditional designs. Stick with similar objects: a pair of Chinese ginger jars or antique silver candlesticks arranged in mirror fashion on either side of the mantel equidistant from the center, for example. Or keep the look simple by placing a single but important object in the center; it could be a mantel clock, a floral arrangement, or some other objet d'art.

Asymmetry, on the other hand, brings a different dynamic to a mantel vignette with mismatched pieces. Try placing a large object to one side of the mantel, and then balance that piece by massing several small objects or a different type of object of similar scale on the opposite side. An example might be an arrangement of books of varying heights and sizes at one end of the mantel and a simple large vase at the other end. Or you might oppose tall thin candlesticks with one fat candle.

Over the Mantel and on the Walls

How much or how little you want to accent the wall just above the mantel depends on how much space there is, the size of the fireplace, and how elaborate your mantel display is. Although a handsome mantelpiece may deserve to stand on its own as an important architectural or decorative feature, in most cases framed art only adds to the appeal of the fireplace by drawing attention to it. However, a framed piece that is too small will look

Plan out all arrangements carefully ahead of time. In general, keep larger items at the bottom so that the overall effect doesn't look top heavy. Before driving any nails into the wall, sketch the arrangement on paper closely if not exactly to scale. Another way is to try out different arrangements of the actual pieces—on the floor. This way you can gauge how the different objects will look on the wall. Before removing them, measure the entire area and draw a box to scale on paper. Then go back to locate and measure the top center of each piece on the floor, and record its appropriate location in the box. A third method is to trace each item onto plain paper, cut out the tracings, and then tape them to the wall, rearranging as you go until you come up with something that looks right.

You can use decorating and arranging tricks to visually alter the dimensions of the fireplace, too. Add the perception of height with vertical

elements such as an arrangement of framed prints that creates a tall vertical line above the mantel. Towering candles on the mantel can reinforce your efforts. If the problem is too much space above the mantel, arrange objects horizontally or hang wall art (mirrors, prints, paints, a clock) low. Choose short fat candles or long horizontal objects that will draw the eye across rather than up. To create the illusion of a wider, more massive hearth, play up the wall to each side of the fireplace by "extending" the surround with molding or furnishings such as bookcases or shelving.

Paint and color are always part of a decorator's bag of tricks. In general, remember that bold, warm colors advance while pale, cool colors recede. For example, make more out of an uninspired surround by painting it a lighter color than the walls. Or paint it a contrasting color. If the walls are a print and you want to de-emphasize the fireplace, paint it the same color as the background of the print. Conversely, if you want to make the fireplace stand out, choose one of the accent colors in the print.

Designer Tip

If you are planning a display of drawings or photography for above or next to your fireplace, choose a frame that is large enough to accommodate a mat. The frame should be 1 to 3 inches larger than the art. Then select a mat that is at least 6 inches larger than the picture for a fresh, updated look.

insignificant over a fireplace. As a rule, the width of the frame should be about two-thirds the width of the mantel. If you still want to hang something smaller, pair it with another object to achieve the most attractive overall scale and proportion.

Also, it's helpful to accent fine art with lighting. A fixture that can be mounted to the top of the frame is one good idea, but recessed spotlights properly focused to highlight a work of art—whether it's wall art or a mantelpiece—can add special drama. Most importantly, the light source should be angled to properly show off the object. Remember, you're using the lamp to draw attention to the artwork, not to the fixture itself.

Sconces are another way to attract attention to the area around a fireplace. Candle sconces look romantic, especially when the candles are lit. Incandescent electric light sconces can have a similar effect, especially if you use shades, which will deflect glare, or a dimmer. For a rich warm glow, use black shades, particularly ones that are lined inside with gold paper.

You can showcase all types of things on a mantel. Ideas include **an heirloom collection** of family photos and old books, opposite; **objects grouped by theme**, such as shells, prints, and a glass bottle representing the sea, above; or a formal **arrangement of antiques**: candlesticks and mercury balls flanking a stately vintage timepiece.

a portfolio of
stylish design

today's technology

Easy, safe, and efficient—three words that **describe** the **benefits** of fireplace technology.

Handsome and romantic, but—drafty. Thirty years ago, you might have described a traditional fireplace in this way. But that was before technological advancements finally made fireplaces more efficient. Now, not only can you expect your fireplace to provide ambiance and warmth, you can relax knowing that your energy dollars aren't going up in smoke. Over the centuries, people had tried to improve the efficiency of the fireplace so that it would generate the maximum heat possible from the wood consumed. But real strides didn't come until the energy crisis of the early 1970s. That's when designers of fireplaces and stoves introduced some significant innovations. Today, fireplaces are not only more efficient, but cleaner and easier to use. Stoves are discussed in Chapter 6; in this chapter, the focus is on fireplaces and all of the improvements and options that are available.

The traditional fireplace is an all-masonry construction, consisting of only bricks and mortar. However, new constructions and reconstructions of masonry fireplaces often include either a metal or a ceramic firebox. This type of firebox has double walls. The space between these walls is where cool air heats up after being drawn in through openings near the floor of the room. The warm air exits through openings near the top of the firebox. Although a metal firebox is more efficient than an all-masonry firebox, it doesn't radiate heat very effectively, and the heat from the fireplace is distributed by convection—that is, the circulation of warmed air. This improvement in heating capacity comes from the warm air emitted by the upper openings. But that doesn't

keep your feet toasty on a cold winter's night—remember, warm air rises.

A more recent development is the ceramic firebox, which is engineered from modern materials such as the type used in kilns. Fires in ceramic fireboxes burn hotter, cleaner, and more efficiently than in all-masonry or metal fireboxes. The main reason is that the back and the walls of a ceramic firebox absorb, retain, and reflect heat effectively. This means that during the time the fire is blazing, more heat radiates into the room than with the other fireboxes. Heat radiation is boosted by the fact that

Old and new fireplaces, opposite and above respectively, can burn cleaner and more efficiently thanks to advancements in design, particularly the firebox.

Designer Tip

At least one or two manufacturers make inserts that will fit the taller and narrower dimensions of the opening on a classic old fireplace—that is, one that was originally constructed before the twentieth century. (See the Resource Guide on page 110 for information.)

most ceramic units are made with thick walls, and so the fire itself is not set as deeply into the hearth as it is with all-masonry or metal fireboxes. As a bonus, because heat is absorbed and retained by the material, the firebox actually radiates a significant amount of heat many hours after the fire has died down. By contrast, a metal firebox cools quickly once the heat source goes out.

In fireplace reconstruction, a metal replacement firebox is usually less expensive than a ceramic one, but the metal does break down over time, in a process professionals refer to as burnout. In addition, an air-circulating metal firebox can only be installed in masonry constructions that already have ports for the intake of cool air and the discharge of warmed air, or in masonry fireplaces in which such ports can be added. On the other hand, ceramic fireboxes can be installed in any type of masonry fireplace and are not subject to burnout.

MANUFACTURED FIREPLACES

The metal fireplaces that are made today can be zero-clearance or freestanding. The zero-clearance units are so named because they can be installed safely against combustible surfaces such as wood. Any of a number of methods are used to keep the outer jacket cool enough, but in general, these fireplaces are designed to use cool air as the primary insulator. Many manufactured fireplaces, including zero-clearance units, are made with fireboxes lined with a refractory material. The chimneys are also made of metal, and a variety of designs use noncombustible material or air as insulation to keep the outer surface at a safe temperature.

The racy red direct-vent unit, above, makes a statement in front of the windows. **A new double-sided fireplace,** opposite, with a ceramic firebox, is versatile and efficient, and enhances two adjacent rooms.

How to Quit Smoking

Before attempting to light a wood fire, make certain that the damper is open all the way. This allows a good draft (flow of air up the chimney) to prevent smoke from blowing back into the room. To ensure a good draft—particularly if your home is well insulated—open a window a bit when lighting a fire.

The opposite of draft is downdraft, which occurs when cold air flows down the chimney and into the room. If the fireplace is properly designed and maintained, the smoke shelf will prevent backpuffing from downdraft most of the time by redirecting cold air currents back up the chimney. The open damper also helps prevent backpuffing.

Also, build a fire slowly to let the chimney liner heat up, which will create a good draft and minimize the chances of downdraft.

The Advantages of a Manufactured Unit

There are some important pluses to choosing a zero-clearance manufactured fireplace. First is the price, which is relatively low, and second, is the easy and quick installation. Also, these units are lightweight and can be installed over almost any type of flooring, including wood. This means they do not need elaborate foundations, which is another cost-saver. Manufactured fireplaces are also extremely efficient, and many are

Today's improvements in design encourage you to indulge in the delights of a fire in many rooms in the house, such as an office, above, or library, opposite.

designed to provide both radiated heat from the firebox and convection heat from ducting.

Manufactured freestanding fireplaces are actually stoves. They are available in an array of colors, finishes, shapes, and sizes. Like zero-clearance factory-built fireplaces, freestanding models are lightweight, offering the same advantages: no need for heavy masonry or additional reinforcement of flooring. And you have a choice of either a wood-burning or gas-powered unit. Heat efficiency is maximized because, in addition to the firebox, the chimney and all sides of the unit radiate heat into the room. Freestanding units may be the least expensive option because installation requires only a chimney hole and, depending on the

type of flooring, a noncombustible pad. A major disadvantage is the space required for placement, because you cannot install most of these units near a combustible wall. Also, a freestanding fireplace is probably not the best choice for families with young children because so much heat is radiated from the exposed surfaces. For more information, see Chapter 6, "The Latest Stoves," beginning on page 84.

Hybrids

If you're looking for a way to get improved efficiency from your older masonry fireplace, consider a gas insert (actually a prefabricated firebox equipped with gas logs). You can purchase either a venting insert or one that's nonventing. But be prepared to pay $1,500 to several thousand dollars for the unit in addition to the cost of installation. For a fraction of that amount you can simply replace real wood logs with ceramic logs powered by gas. Like inserts, these logs may or may not require venting. Consult an experienced plumber or heating contractor, and remember that once you convert to gas you cannot burn wood.

Improving an old masonry fireplace on the inside by installing a metal firebox might also be an inspiration to update the face and mantel. Pairing two or more finishing materials, such as metal and masonry, can make your fireplace a hybrid in more than one way. For example, combine a stone base with a metal hood and chimney to

create a custom-designed fireplace that works as a room divider in a large space. The design options in terms of materials and technology are seemingly endless.

If you have plans for building an innovative custom design, carefully review them with an expert in fireplace construction and maintenance to make sure you're not doing something hazardous. Also, don't forget to check with your local building inspector so that you don't waste time and money on a project that may not comply with codes and regulations set forth where you live.

ENHANCING THE BASICS

You can improve the efficiency of any manufactured fireplace, and of masonry and hybrid constructions as well, with a few extras. In existing masonry fireplaces, a device commonly referred to as a fresh-air intake accessory or an outside air kit may improve peformance. A fresh-air accessory makes use of outside air instead of heated room air for combustion, thus improving the fireplace's efficiency. There is another way to make your fireplace more efficient that isn't high tech at all, however. Simply replace the grate or firebasket with a superior design—one that provides greater air circulation and allows a better placement of logs. Another type, a heat-exchanger grate, works with a fan. The device draws in the room's air, re-heats it quickly, and then forces it back into the room.

Capitalizing on Technology

Wood is the traditional fuel for a fireplace, and today's manufactured fireplaces offer designs that make the most out of your cord of hardwood. However, wood is not the only fuel option. In fact, in some places, it's not an option

An old exposed brick chimney, opposite, is charming when it's combined with a refurbished facade. One way to upgrade an existing older fireplace, above, is with an energy-efficient fireplace insert.

at all. There are manufactured units that offer a choice of natural gas or propane as a fuel source, which heats ceramic logs designed to realistically simulate wood. The fire, complete with glowing embers, is often difficult to distinguish from one burning real wood.

In some areas of the country, fireplace emission regulations have become strict—in places such as much of Colorado and parts of Nevada and California, so strict that new construction of wood-burning fireplaces has been outlawed. In these areas, manufactured units using alternative fuels allow homeowners all the benefits of a wood-burning fireplace without the adverse impact on air quality.

Most of the units available today also offer a variety of amenities, including built-in thermostatic control and remote-control devices for turning the fire on and off and regulating heat output.

Don't wait until fall to inspect the chimney. Do this job, or call a chimney sweep, when the weather is mild. Because some repairs take a while to make, it's best to have them done when the fireplace is not normally in use. If you do the inspection yourself, wear old clothes, eye goggles, and a mask.

MORE HELPFUL IDEAS

HOW TO FIND A CHIMNEY SWEEP

You can purchase tools for removing creosote from flues and chimneys at many home improvement centers, but the expertise to perform a thorough, efficient chimney cleaning is more than most homeowners can safely take on. A professional, experienced chimney sweep can do the job quickly—usually in less than 2 hours. In addition, a professional knows what to look for to make sure all parts of the fireplace or stove are in safe working order. He or she can identify problems—such as cracks in masonry, broken flue tiles, or warped joints in stovepipes or metal chimney liners—that are potential hazards.

To find a good chimney sweep, you can look in the "Yellow Pages," but it's better to seek recommendations from other homeowners. Better yet, inquire about a chimney sweep in your area through the National Chimney Sweep Guild. Certified members agree to adhere to the guild's code of ethics. (see page 114 of the Resource Guide.)

THE IMPORTANCE OF A CLEAN SWEEP

Finally, one of the most important factors in the use of a fireplace or stove is the regular inspection and cleaning of the stovepipe, flue, and chimney. To understand why, remember that the burning of wood results in the combustion of solids as well as combustible gases. However, not everything that goes into the firebox is burned, no matter how efficient the appliance. One of the byproducts of wood burning is the dark brown or black tar called creosote, a flammable substance that sticks to the linings of flues and chimneys.

Although the burning temperature of creosote is high, it can ignite and cause a chimney fire. It may be brief and without apparent damage, but a chimney fire may also be prolonged or intense and result in significant fire and smoke damage or, at worst, the loss of your home if the creosote buildup is great enough. Creosote causes other problems, too. It decreases the inside diameter of stovepipes and flues, causing slower burning. This makes burning less efficient and contributes to further deposits of creosote. In addition, because creosote is acidic, it corrodes mortar, metal, and eventually even stainless-steel and ceramic chimney liners.

To prevent costly and dangerous creosote buildup, have your chimney professionally cleaned by a qualified chimney sweep. How often depends on the amount of creosote deposited during the burning season, and this, in turn, depends largely on how and what kind of wood you burn. Professional sweeps usually recommend at least annual cleaning. Depending on where you live, you'll spend about $150, perhaps less, for a cleaning.

Keep the home fires burning safely and cleanly by making sure the chimney flue is clear and there are no cracks in masonry. Do an annual inspection yourself, or leave the job to a professional chimney sweep.

a portfolio of
stylish design

5
outdoor
fire

Even the tiniest **corner on a deck** or
patio can accommodate one of
today's **glowing fire** options.

The warmth and glow of a fire can be alluring whether you are enjoying it indoors or under the open sky. Anyone who has relaxed next to an open campfire in the woods, beside a lake or running brook, or at the beach knows just how pleasant and special the experience can be. That's why so many homeowners are incorporating fire—in the form of an outdoor fireplace, fire pit, heater, or chiminea—into their landscaping plans. Any one of these options can serve as the focal point in a cozy open-air environment where you can enjoy evenings outdoors with friends or family under the stars amid the natural sounds of the night. Besides a welcoming glow, these devices also provide heat and a means for cooking on your patio or deck or in your yard well into the fall and earlier in the spring, times usually regarded as off-season in most places. As the trend toward spending more time outside the house continues, expect to see more variety in the products and options available. In addition to the custom route, the marketplace offers stock, kit, and ready-made fireplaces, fire pits, chimineas, and heaters available in a wide choice of styles, colors, designs, extra options, and prices. In this chapter, you will find an overview of some one-of-a-kind styles as well as what you can expect to find at home improvement or garden centers and on-line. Of course, always remember to use caution with fire, indoors or out. Keep combustible materials, such as wood and fabrics, away from the danger sparks pose, and always make sure to keep an eye on children—as well as the fire—at all times.

OUTDOOR FIREPLACES

Although some prefabricated outdoor fireplaces sell for just a few hundred dollars, usually they represent the greatest opportunity for extravagance in outdoor fire equipment. The options include both freestanding models and units built into a permanent structure such as a stone wall. The fuel sources for either type include wood, natural or propane gas, pellets, or an alcohol-based combustible gel. Just like indoor fireplaces, outdoor units consist of a firebox, hearth, and flue. Some models give off more heat than others, but don't expect to bask in much warmth if you're sitting away from the fire at the far end of a spacious patio or deck. For ambiance and design sophistication, an outdoor fireplace is hard to beat. Keep in mind you'll have to install a drainage system to manage rainwater that can otherwise put a damper on your enjoyment.

An outdoor masonry fireplace can be finished in any style or echo vernacular architecture, such as the stone patio hearth (left) typical of the Northeast or the stucco version (opposite) in Southern California. **A fire pit,** below, takes on an Arts and Crafts look.

Designer Tip

At least one manufacturer makes a see-through, direct-vent, indoor/outdoor gas fireplace. It's installed something like a window and lets you see outdoors when you're inside, and indoors when you're outside. It's also less expensive to install than a masonry fireplace.

work on an outdoor fireplace, check with your building department, which may not allow the installation.

Chimineas

Also called patio fireplaces, traditional chimineas are clay containers that resemble Mexican bread ovens dating back to the seventeenth century. They are well suited for a patio or terrace and come in a range of sizes to suit small or large spaces.

As an outdoor heat and fire source, chimineas are currently enjoying widespread popularity among homeowners. They are relatively inexpensive, with most ranging in price from about $100 to about $300, although some higher-priced models are also on the market. Because of their growth in popularity, you can find chimineas in a variety of retail stores, including lawn and garden centers, home improvement centers, and even shopper's club outlets. They have a characteristic all-in-one design, with a potbellied base tapering above to form

Freestanding outdoor fireplaces often feature a four-sided or circular design so that you can view the fire from wherever you're sitting. Heat emanates from all around this type of unit. Built-in styles have traditional appeal and allow for the maximum opportunity for setting a style because they have a façade. Finishing materials include real or faux brick or stone, stucco, and tile.

The cost of an outdoor fireplace is generally higher than that of other types of outdoor fire and heating units and depends, of course, on how extravagant the design and optional amenities such as façade materials are. Nevertheless, it is possible to find some freestanding metal units for as low as around $300. Before getting to

Prefabricated wood-burning outdoor fireplaces, such as the one pictured above, can closely resemble a masonry unit built by hand. **A chiminea,** right, is a popular alternative today. Traditional clay models must be cured before use, however, or they will crack under high heat.

Preparing to Use a Clay Chiminea

Before getting started, there are a couple of general rules about using a clay chiminea. Make sure the chiminea is completely dry before lighting a fire, or else it will crack. Also, line the bottom of the pot with about 4 inches of sand. Finally, always build the fire slowly, and never use kerosene or charcoal lighter fluid.

To cure a new clay chiminea, follow these simple steps:

● Build a small paper fire inside the pot. For kindling, use strips of newspaper rolled into a few balls. Place one newspaper ball on the sand inside the chiminea. Ignite it with a match. Then add another ball, and another, one at a time, until the outside walls of the chiminea are slightly warm. Allow the fire to burn out; then let the pot cool completely before the next step.

● Once the chiminea feels cool, light another small fire, this time using wood. Again, let the fire burn out naturally, and then allow the unit to completely cool.

● Repeat the process of lighting a wood fire three more times, adding more kindling and building a larger fire with each consecutive attempt. Remember to let the chiminea cool completely between fires. After the fifth fire, the chiminea should be cured and ready to use anytime you want a cozy fire.

a circular flue. The potbelly, with a hearthlike opening, is known as the fire bowl, and the flue is referred to as the chimney pipe. If you live in a climate where you can't leave clay outside during the winter, choose one of today's designs crafted in sturdy cast iron or aluminum. But even these should be covered with a heavy plastic during the off-season.

Almost all chimineas use wood as the fuel source, but at

This custom-built natural stone fireplace, left, blends in beautifully with the surrounding wall and patio, and almost appears to be a part of the landscape. **Another one-of-a-kind example,** above, has been fashioned in stucco. The color of the painted fireplace wall picks up the clay tiles and makes it the dramatic focal point of this custom-designed outdoor oasis.

least one manufacturer has introduced a model that burns either propane or natural gas. Because the fire bowl openings on most wood-burning models are smaller than those you'd find in standard woodstoves, the wood has to be cut smaller than is usual. Other fuel options now include aromatic woods, including those that emit an insect-repellant smoke when burned. The latest technology also features an igniter and a manual control that lets you adjust the flame from high to low. Although some chimineas come outfitted with a cooking grate, they're essentially just for adding atmosphere to an outdoor area.

If you plan to use a chiminea on a deck, place a heat-proof deck mat under it. These are available in a variety of fireproof materials, although most are made of metal. Surfaces such as stone may not require heat protection. Regardless of the surface on which the chiminea will sit, a

spark screen is an important safety accessory for wood-burning models. Just as in a standard fireplace, wood may snap, crackle, and pop out red hot particles of various sizes through the opening in the chiminea's fire bowl. Spark screens are readily available wherever chimineas are sold.

FIRE PITS

Gas-fueled fire pits were first marketed for people who wanted to enjoy a campfire in areas where outdoor wood fires were banned, either because of the high risk of forest fires or because of air-quality issues. Gradually, interest in these devices has heated up as people who don't have the desire or space for a fireplace have discovered that they can still have the charm of a fire in their own backyard. In addition to their aesthetic appeal, some firepits come with accessories, such as a barbecue grill, kettle hook, and spark screen. Plus, many of them are lightweight, which means you can take them with you to the beach or campsite. Fire pits that come with wheels let you move the units to any side of the deck or patio. If you wish, you can have a fire pit that is permanently installed as well.

Designs vary. Some are built to resemble an actual campfire, complete with faux rocks ringing a set of burning logs. Manufacturers of this type of fire pit often disguise the propane tank under faux rocks or logs. Some companies offer a central pit with a gas-burning log set surrounded by a table or a bench. The newest innovation is the placement of a gas-burning log set in a kettle container.

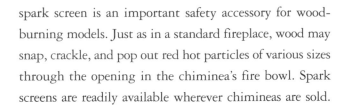

A deck is a perfect spot for a fire pit, such as the custom-built brick examples in the redwood decks pictured above left and opposite, especially if you extend your outdoor activities into the evening. **Other types of fire pits** include models that you can buy. A copper finish adds glamour to the one at left, which uses gel alcohol as its fuel.

Patio Heaters

Patio heaters were once used only commercially in warmer climates—at restaurants, inns, and resorts—to heat outdoor recreation and dining areas on cool evenings. In recent years, homeowners have discovered the practicality and satisfaction of extending the usable time of their outdoor living spaces by installing a patio heater. A number of manufacturers have recently introduced a line of patio heaters designed in particular for home use. If you plan to spend a lot of time outdoors in the evening, you might want to add one of these stylish units—even as a supplement to an outdoor fireplace.

The most common type of patio heater consists of a heating element housed within a dome. The dome, in turn, sits atop a pole, and the propane tank—the fuel source—is housed in the base. A typical patio heater delivers heat within about a 15- to 20-foot radius. Units made for home use usually are designed for portability and can be easily moved to the garage or storage shed when they're not needed.

A recent innovation is an infrared heater that is mounted on the house or awning rather than on a pole. Other variations in the freestanding floor design include models mounted on a pole that fits through the "umbrella hole" on a patio table.

With the number of manufacturers offering these units today, the choices in design and color accommodate a variety of tastes and preferences. Prices vary according to features offered, including such options as remote-control operation, but a basic unit may carry a retail price as low as around $200.

If your outdoor space can't accommodate a full-size fireplace, such as the one pictured on the opposite page, there are affordable, practical alternatives. **A patio heater,** left and above, may come freestanding to suit a spacious deck or patio, or as a tabletop unit, which is ideal for a small porch or an intimate dining area.

a portfolio of stylish design

the latest stoves

The **newest** units offer color, style, and fuel choices, **advanced** design, plus venting and nonventing **options**.

For homeowners who desire a fireplace in an existing structure but don't want to go through the considerable expense of having a contractor break through walls to install one, a freestanding stove represents an attractive solution. It may also be an alternative to a fireplace for environmental, budgetary, or design reasons. And you won't have to sacrifice the pleasure of watching a crackling fire on a cool night if you choose a stove, either. Many models are made with a generous-sized glass front, creating a hearthlike effect. Gas, electric, or wood-burning stove inserts offer the benefits of today's technology, and allow you to convert an old masonry fireplace into a model of efficient design. But for many people, whether the unit is a traditional wood-burning device or powered by gas or pellet-burning products, the inviting look of a freestanding stove captures its own unique charm. Besides appearance, an efficient stove offers warmth, and depending on the unit, heat enough to keep you toasty on cold winter days. In this chapter, you'll find examples of various types of stoves and learn about the options for fuel and installation. To start you thinking about the virtues of a stove, you might enjoy a bit of background information regarding stoves, then and now.

The modern wood-burning stove was an invention born of necessity. Around the middle of the eighteenth century, Benjamin Franklin became concerned about the shortage of firewood in and around Philadelphia. This inspired his own stove design, which was made of iron and was somewhat cube-shaped, with an opening at the front sufficiently large to allow a view of the fire. Franklin also included in his stove a device that could be used to

close off the opening to keep too much air from being drawn into the firebox, allowing for more efficient burning of less wood. His later design improvements included modifications to the airflow so that the particles and combustible gases in smoke were also burned. Another innovation in Franklin's design was the addition of an "air box" that drew cool air from the cellar, heated it, and then directed the warm air currents toward the corners of the room.

Two centuries later—during the oil embargo and resulting energy crisis of the 1970s—the rapid increase in petroleum fuel prices led to new interest in wood-burning stoves as a source of heat. The stove and fireplace industry grew quickly, and new research and development efforts led to important innovations in both stove and fireplace designs.

Brick, stone, and concrete are all attractive options for creating a handsome setting that protects the wall from the heat of a stove. Unless the unit is gas-powered, you might also need a bottom heat shield for the floor.

Designer Tip

An electric stove offers lots of cozy ambiance, and it can be installed anywhere in the house. All you need to install one of these units is access to an outlet. Today's electric stoves also simulate a burning fire realistically without the concerns of some other types of stoves.

AS OF TODAY

Today's freestanding stoves are made of steel, stone, or cast iron, and the variety of finishes is impressive. You can find stoves to accent or blend with any architectural or decorating style, from the formal living room to a child-centered family room. Finishes for metal stoves come in enamel or porcelain, in a range of colors. In addition, surrounds and mantels can be added as decorative elements (keeping in mind, of course, the clearance requirements of the particular stove).

The array of style choices is also bountiful and includes variations on period or nostalgic looks as well sleek contemporary designs. In addition to different stove shapes and dimensions, decorative details vary.

Cleaner and More Efficient

A stove installation requires no major changes to an existing structure, with the exception of the addition of a chimney. (Electric and some gas stoves do not need a chimney.) Another important economic advantage—and perhaps the most significant one—is a stove's capability as a heating unit. Even the most efficient modern fireplaces lose a significant amount of heat up the chimney, but not so with stoves. Advancements over the past 25 years have made stoves cleaner, more efficient burners of fuel, consuming smaller quantities of fuel and releasing less pollution into the air. The wood-burning stoves sold in the United States since July 1, 1992, must meet the Environmental Protection Agency's standards for the acceptable level of byproducts that go up the chimney. All EPA-certified woodstoves are labeled as such. By law, labels also must show the emission levels for that product (shown in grams of particulates emitted per hour), the efficiency level, and the heat output value (how many BTUs the stove can put out per hour). A woodstove's label also must show whether it

Stoves come in all types: European-sleek and gas-fueled, top left; Victorian-styled pellet-burning, left; or an old-fashioned-looking woodstove, opposite, equipped with the latest, safest, and most efficient technology.

has a catalytic or noncatalytic combustion system.

Catalytic Combustors. A catalytic combustor is a device made of a ceramic material and coated with a rare metal, usually platinum or palladium. A catalytic combustor lowers the temperature at which smoke will ignite and burn, so in these systems, smoke that is released when the wood burns is directed into a catalytic combustion chamber rather than being released directly into the air. In the chamber, much of the particulate matter is burned, so fewer particulates are released.

In addition to the environmental benefits, stoves with a catalytic combustor are more cost-effective because the particulates serve as a kind of "bonus fuel" that ignites in the catalytic chamber, providing additional heat. A cleaner burn also means that less creosote is produced, reducing the amount of this sticky, flammable substance that adheres to the insides of chimneys. This, in turn,

---

A gas or wood-burning stove insert can transform what was an old heat-losing traditional masonry fireplace, above, into a model of efficiency and convenience.

also lowers the risk of fire igniting in the chimney.

Noncatalytic Stoves. Noncatalytic stoves also have a second chamber outside the firebox to which smoke is directed. But instead of lowering smoke's kindling point, the noncatalytic chamber has higher temperatures to ignite the smoke. Noncatalytic stoves certified by the EPA are significantly more efficient than previous models, although they generally are less efficient than catalytic stoves.

Fuel Options

Stoves are made to burn wood logs, gas, coal, wood pellets, or oil. Wood is still the most popular fuel option for two main reasons: it's relatively inexpensive in most areas of the country, and the look, ambiance, and aroma of burning logs make an attractive combination of features. However, some local regulations restrict or even outlaw wood burning. But other options exist, and you should consider them.

Gas is the most convenient alternative to wood. A gas stove provides instant heat and a fire that doesn't require

Stove Safety

A couple of issues need special emphasis with regard to stoves. The first is protecting children from contact burns. Several manufacturers make sturdy fireproof safety screens.

The second issue is making sure that logs are the right length to fit into the firebox. Once a log that's too long is popped into a hot stove, removing it safely can be tricky. Seasoned logs catch fire quickly. Nevertheless, should you insert a log that's too long in the stove, remove it immediately and transport it in a fireproof container (such as a metal ashcan) to a safe place outside: a gravel driveway, a sandbox, or a stone or concrete patio. Remember that a scorched log may be slowly burning, even if you can't see smoke. A dousing with water from a bucket or garden hose will help.

Inadvertently closing a glass door on a slightly oversized log represents a whole set of hazards: broken glass, the need to remove the log, and a fire burning without a protective barrier between it and the combustibles in the room. If there are only embers in the firebox or the fire is low-burning and small, remove the log as described above and close what's left of the door. Open some windows, and let the fire burn down naturally. Then smother the embers with cold ashes from your ash bucket or with sand. If the fire is still crackling and sparking, create a fireproof barrier in front of the opening to prevent sparks from shooting onto combustible materials. (Possibilities for makeshift screens include metal cookie sheets or an all-metal window screen propped against the stove front.) Make sure the embers have burned out.

If there are shooting sparks and flames, get children out and call the fire department. While you wait, try to contain the flames in the firebox. (Throwing water on a fire is a last resort because of the steam and smoke that will result.) Don't cancel the SOS to the fire department even if it looks as if the flames are out.

attention to keep the flames going. As a bonus, there are no ashes to sweep. Some gas models (direct-vent) are vented directly to the outdoors without the use of a chimney. Others (nonventing) don't require venting, but some states outlaw their use. However, it's important to remember that along with the convenience of gas comes a higher cost.

Some wood-burning stoves can be adapted to burn coal. There are manufacturers who offer wood-burning models with special grate inserts that convert the stove to a coal burner, so the same stove can burn either fuel. A cost-effective alternative to burning wood logs is to use pellets made of materials such as wood waste and sawdust. Other clean and efficient so-called biomass fuels include pellets processed from materials such as corn kernels.

A centrally located stove can be an efficient way to add heat and style to an open-plan layout. The model at left is sleek and modern, in keeping with the home's design.

a portfolio of stylish design

7
tools and accessories

Accessories for fireplaces and stoves can make **tending the fire** safe, **stylish,** and efficient.

Y ou'll need a few specific tools and accessories to make using your fireplace or wood-burning stove convenient and safe. Other items are certainly not required but are handy and helpful (a damper hanger), decorative (an ornate cast-iron fireback), or just plain fun (a traditional popcorn popper—a favorite of both kids and adults). You can purchase these things from a variety of sources, including specialty catalogs and stores, crafts shows (particularly those that feature the work of blacksmiths), home improvement centers, malls, antique stores, the classified ads in your local newspaper, the Internet, and even general merchandise discount stores. Some items can be custom-made, but these come at a higher cost, of course. Hand-forged and hand-cast items are attractive and may come in special finishes such as verdigris, silver or gold leaf, antique pewter, chrome, polished brass, or bronze. But even off-the-shelf items are offered in a variety of finishes, configurations, and styles.

Where it's appropriate, you may also want to be creative, finding use for unexpected items rather than conventional things with which to accessorize. An example might be making use of an old metal box to house logs or kindling. As long as what you choose gets the job done effectively and safely, it's fine, and you won't have to sacrifice personal style. In this chapter, you'll find an overview of what equipment you need along with a variety of related items that, while not necessities, can enhance the way you live with and enjoy your fire.

Designer Tip

Professionals recommend keeping glass doors open while a fire is burning. When the doors are left completely open, the burning flame has a more realistic appearance and the glass doesn't become soiled by swirling ashes. When the doors are closed, heat from a large hot fire can break the glass.

THE BASICS

Although you'll probably store most of the season's logs outdoors, you can keep handy a sufficient supply of dry wood indoors. You'll need pieces of various sizes, from small, fast-burning kindling to long-burning, hefty logs. The most convenient place to store the woodpile is near the fireplace or stove, and a number of manufacturers make wood holders from metal or wood in a range of sizes. One of the most functional, sturdiest, and safest holders for hearthside use is a metal rack. Metal racks are available in several styles—with or without decorative accents—including space-efficient U- and circular shapes. Many fireplace and stove users also prefer

A sturdy basket, above, stands in suitably for log storage, but a metal rack with wheels, right, makes transporting firewood from outdoors easier. **When choosing a grate,** such as the one featured inside the firebox opposite, let weight be an indicator of quality.

the convenience of log-carrying and storage sets. One of these sets consists of a sturdy, yet lightweight canvas or leather carrying bag for toting wood and a container that lets you store the filled tote.

For kindling, you could use a kindling box or metal container designed specifically for this purpose. But you may prefer something different, such as a restored antique toy chest, a child's wagon, or just a simple wicker basket. Actually it could be anything as long as you keep it safely away from the fireplace or stove to prevent a fire caused by sparking. Old wooden chests and baskets are charming but flammable.

Polished brass andirons, like the ones on the opposite page, are elegant, but their lacquer finish can be damaged by harsh cleaning agents. It's best to clean them with a liquid soap solution. **Even wrought iron,** above, calls for gentle nonabrasive treatment.

Grate Ideas

To ignite a fire and keep it burning in a fireplace, you have to elevate the logs off the hearth floor so that air can flow underneath them. That's what a grate is for. Essentially, it is a metal cradle for logs. Usually nothing more than four short legs connected by a frame and a series of metal crosspieces, it's simple but functional.

Andirons. A set of andirons is another support for the logs. Crafted of metal, an andiron consists of a vertical shaft attached to a horizontal bar mounted on short legs. Usually the vertical shaft is decorative, ranging from a simple ball-topped finial to animal heads and other designs. Used in pairs, andirons are placed with the shaft at the front of the hearth and the horizontal bar perpendicular to the back wall; the logs are laid cross-wise. A really fine set can be handsome—and pricey. You may want to consider an antique pair, which you can find at auctions or antique stores. Sometimes you can

spot a venerable set in chrome or wrought iron at a reasonable price if you browse the Internet or frequent thrift shops and yard sales. Admirers of modern design can find andirons fashioned in chrome in graphic, bold shapes. Old or new, andirons can be unique and stylish, so look for ones that in form and finish complement your decorating scheme—be it rustic, traditional, contemporary, or country.

Radiating Warmth

If you have a standard masonry fireplace, you probably know that much of the heat goes up the chimney, not into the room. A vertical metal accessory known as a fireback can help conserve some of the heat that would otherwise escape outdoors. A fireback sits behind the burning logs and absorbs heat from the fire, then radiates it into the room. As a bonus, it may protect stone, brick, and mortar from soot. Antique cast-iron firebacks with classic ornamental designs are occasional lucky finds at barn and yard sales, especially in rural areas. An alternative to a fireback, but serving the same function, is a specially designed, three-panel reflector, which is also suitable for use behind a gas log set.

MORE STANDARD GEAR TO CONSIDER

Whether you have a fireplace or stove, you need some standard tools to manage the flames, embers, and ash. Keeping the fire burning means occasionally manipulating or poking the logs and stirring the embers to knock off the ash, which can smother a fire. For this purpose, nothing beats two basic uten-

Choose tools that complement your decor. Moorish-looking andirons, above, seem fitting when paired with Old World tiles. **A simple iron-handled brush** and damper hook appear suitably rustic against the stone hearth, left, while **classic motifs** on the screen and ball finials on the tool set grace a formal fireplace, opposite.

Designer Tip

If you live near the ocean, you must take extra precautions to protect the baked-on enamel finish that often accompanies fireplace accessories. Periodically apply natural bee's wax. Buff the finish with a soft, clean, dry cloth. Do this between waxings, and don't over-wax or the buildup will trap dirt.

sils: a poker and log tongs. And a few puffs from a set of bellows is often all that's needed to motivate sluggish embers or a smoldering log to burst into flames.

Later, after the fire has gone out, removing cold ash from the hearth is easily accomplished with a broom and shovel. (Owners of gas units don't have to worry about this, however.) These tools are so frequently used that they're usually sold, with a holder, in matched sets as a decorative accessory unit. Styles run the gamut from the clean and simple lines of basic wrought iron to elegant brass with ornately cast handles and finials.

Screens & Boards

A wire mesh fireplace screen can protect the room and its furnishings from sparks. You can find freestanding models (hinged panels or one flat piece) or the type that is called a curtain screen because it hangs from a metal frame and opens and closes in the center. The important thing is to make sure that whatever style you choose, the screen is the right size to cover the hearth opening sufficiently.

A fire board is an attractive solution to covering the black hole when a fireplace is not in use, such as during the summer months. The Victorians loved them. A fire board is typically made of wood, although it can also be constructed of fabric or even paper, so you can't use it when

Screens can be utilitarian or decorative. Metal mesh sceens (left and opposite) protect against sparks. But the wooden folding screen, below, is only decorative.

Damper Plaques

Is the damper open or closed? Depending on how the damper in your fireplace is rigged, you have to either raise or lower the handle, or pull down or let up on a chain. Knowing the position of the damper makes the difference between whether you start a nice, cozy fire or a create a smoky mess in the living room. Fortunately, there's a way to keep track without having to crawl around on the hearth with a flashlight: damper memory joggers.

The least expensive version of this solution is a small metal plaque embossed with "Damper Open" on one side and "Damper Closed" on the other. Also available are damper hangers, ranging from simple cast-iron filigree designs to elaborate brass renderings. They hook onto the end of the damper handle when the damper is closed.

the fireplace is lit. A fire board is strictly decorative, but like a fire screen, a fire board can consist of hinged panels or one flat panel that is mounted into a frame. You can easily make one. See the instructions on the opposite page.

Glass doors are another option. In addition to protecting a room from sparks, glass doors also keep the heat in the room from escaping through the chimney. Glass doors let you see the fire, and tinted or etched versions camouflage the black hole when the fire is out. There are various styles, framed and frameless, that are suitable for traditional as well as contemporary interiors. Again, getting a proper fit over the opening is essential, so take measurements before you shop. If your hearth is an odd shape or size, discuss having a custom glass door fabricated by a local glass cutter.

Another safeguard against spark damage on floors is a hearth rug. The ideal hearth rug is made of wool, which is naturally fire-resistant and won't "melt down" if a long-lived spark or ember lands on it. However, wool rugs can be pricey. Rugs made with synthetic materials and treated with a flame-retardant chemical are less expensive. The down side of the synthetics is that, although they will not catch fire, they can scorch and fibers can be damaged. Sizes, shapes (round, half-round, rectangular), and color varieties are often limited in anything other than fireplace specialty stores, so you might have to shop around to find the combination you want.

Beyond the Pail

Unless you have a fireplace or stove equipped with an ash chute to the basement, you'll need to manually remove the ashes from the hearth or firebox. The shovel and broom that come with a standard fireplace tool set work fine, but you'll also need an ash can in which to put the ashes and carry them outside for safe disposal. Styles range from a basic small galvanized metal cylindrical can with a lid and

Rugs and other furnishings near the hearth should not be flammable. A stone ledge, above, and stone in front of the fireplace, right, make it possible to keep the glass doors open safely without worrying about sparks.

HOW TO MAKE A HINGED FIRE BOARD

You'll need a hinged three-panel wooden fireplace screen, which you can buy or make. If you buy one, you'll have to sand and prime it thoroughly before applying the new finish over the existing one. Ideally, it's best to work on unfinished wood.

The screen used for this project features two 9 x 36-inch side panels and one 26 x 36-inch center panel that were cut from a ¾-inch-thick sheet of plywood. If you aren't handy with a circular saw or table saw, ask your local lumber supplier to cut the panels to your desired dimensions. Attach the side and center panels with two-way (piano) hinges, which are easy to install. Simply mark their location along the inside edges of the panel pieces, drill pilot holes, and then screw the hinges into place. To finish, prime the boards, then paint or stencil a design onto each panel. For Victorian authenticity, decoupage the panels with a motif cut out of a piece of fabric, wallpaper, old greeting cards, or postcards.

handle to more elegant buckets—such as a boat-shaped ash bucket with decorative accents—that you don't have to hide away between sweepings.

A specialty appliance, a warm ash vacuum, is available for those who prefer a fast and neat cleanup. A fireproof canister holds warm ashes deposited by a flame-resistant hose.

MATCHLESS CONVENIENCE

Getting a fire going on a cold hearth can be time-consuming. To make it easier, a number of manufacturers market fire-starting aids. For example, as an alternative to kindling (twigs and small branches) that you have to gather outdoors, you can buy boxes of fatwood. Fatwood is cut from pine stumps after logging and, because it contains a high amount of highly flammable pine resin, it catches fire readily and burns quickly and hot.

A manufactured version of the same idea are fire-starter logs, consisting of waste sawdust and wax, compressed and formed into rectangular blocks. Like fatwood, these fire-starter logs ignite quickly and burn long enough to get the fire going. "Designer" starters can also be found in gift catalogs and other outlets. These are made in the same way and work on the same principle as less fancy starter logs but come in decorative shapes (stars or acorns, for example) and may be scented with pine, cinnamon, or another aroma.

Cape cod lighters are less expensive to use than fatwood or fire-starter logs. These are small metal pots—usually cast iron—with a porous pumice ball on a metal wand. You pour kerosene or lamp oil into the pot and submerge the pumice ball. Then you lay the pumice ball, which soaks up a small amount of the flammable liquid, on the hearth beneath the logs and ignite it with a match. The flame burns long enough to get wood burning.

Home Comforts

For a charming, old-fashioned family night at home that stokes the imagination, hearth cooking is hard to beat. With the broad array of special vessels and utensils available, it's possible to create culinary wonders on the open hearth—everything from soup to nuts, literally. Popcorn poppers, hearth forks for cooking hot dogs or shish kebabs (and toasting marshmallows later), and a hanging stew pot are but a few of the possibilities. And as fireplaces have become safer, cleaner, and easier to operate, more utensils and devices for enjoying them in this way have been introduced. If you think you'd like to cook with your new prefabricated fireplace, you should ask about the extra equipment you can purchase when you're shopping.

Easy Care

Flame-resistant leather or suede gloves are a handy addition to the fireplace tool chest. Donning them allows you to safely load more wood onto an already-roaring fire or to quickly retrieve a log or hot ember that escapes from the firebox.

If you have children, keeping them a safe distance away from the stove or open hearth is always a concern. Options include a steel mesh screen or a metal gate system with a latched entry door. The latter is particularly sturdy and is suitable for homes with determined toddlers. Finally, wall-mounted designs are available for match safes, containers for matches that protect the match heads from accidentally igniting. Some are copies of antique designs once highly popular in Victorian parlors. Floor-standing match holders also serve the purpose, and range from tall cylinders for long matches to metal holders cast in imaginative designs.

Utensils lend an old-fashioned flavor to a fire, above. In a family room, left, there's room to toast marshmallows. Opposite, even without a fire, this hearth is appealing.

a portfolio of stylish design

resource guide

The following list of manufacturers and associations is meant to be a general guide to additional industry and product-related sources. It is not intended as a listing of products and manufacturers represented by the photographs in this book.

Aladdin Hearth Products *manufactures the Quadra-Fire line of home heating systems that include clean-burning hearth appliances, freestanding stoves, gas fireplaces, and gas, wood, and pellet inserts.*
Phone: 800-234-2508
Fax: 800-546-4474
1445 North Hwy.
Colville, WA 99114-2008
www.quadrafire.com

Aloha Fireplaces *specializes in custom fireplaces, fireplace tile, and accessories.*
7655 E. Evans Rd.
Scottsdale, AZ 85260
Phone: 480-922-1042
www.alohafireplace.com

American Gas Association (AGA) *represents 189 local natural gas utilites. These companies deliver gas to 54 million businesses and homes all across the United States. AGA offers information for the consumer about energy efficiency and appliances.*
400 N. Capital St. N.W.
Washington, DC 20001
Phone: 202-824-7000
Fax: 202-824-7115
www.aga.org

Buckley Rumford Fireplaces *is a source for Rumford fireplaces, fireplace parts and other related products, and dealers.*
1035 Monroe St.
Port Townsend, WA 98368
Phone: 360-385-9974
www.rumford.com

California Redwood Association *is the trade association for redwood lumber producers. It offers design advice and redwood lumber sources.*
405 Enfrente Dr.
Novato, CA 94949
Phone: 415-382-0662
www.calred.org

Central Fireplace *manufactures gas fireplaces, freestanding stoves, gas inserts, and child-proof remote controls.*
20502 160th St.
Greenbush, MN 56726
Phone: 800-248-4681
Fax: 218-782-2580
www.centralfireplace.com

C.J.'s Home Decor & Fireplaces *sells and installs grill and hearth products for indoor and outdoor use.*
120 Stryker Ln., Suite 209
Hillsborough, NJ 08844
Phone: 888-986-1535
Fax: 908-904-1575
www.fireplacesandgrills.com

Cumberland Woodcraft Company *is a retailer of handcrafted Victorian-style fireplace mantels, corbels, bars, millwork, and hardwood carvings among other things.*
P.O. Drawer 609
Carlisle, PA 17013-0609
Phone: 717-243-0063
www.cumberlandwoodcraft.com

Dancing Fire, Inc. *is a company specializing in the sale of chimineas and Pinion firewood, which is ideal for aromatic chiminea fires.*
Phone: 817-613-0029
Fax: 817-594-0039
www.dancingfire.com

resource guide

Duraflame, Inc. *makes firelogs, fire-starters, and related accessories for indoor and outdoor fireplaces.*
P.O. Box 1230
Stockton, CA 95201
Phone: 800-342-2896
Fax: 209-462-9412
www.duraflame.com

Endless Summer Patio Heaters *sells residential, commercial, and tabletop heaters for outdoor use. The company also sells outdoor wood-burning fireplaces. Endless Summer is an affiliate of The UniFlame Corporation.*
Phone: 800-762-1142
Fax: 847-731-6032
www.uniflame.com/patio_heaters/

Final Touches *is a retailer of chimineas and related accessories.*
115 Morris St.
Blowing Rock, NC 28605
Phone: 877-506-2741
www.chiminea.net

Fire Designs *manufactures fireplace-related products.*
310 N. Michigan Ave.
Suite 200
Chicago, IL 60601-3702
Phone: 800-661-4788
Fax: 312-263-5855
www.firedesigns.net

Fires of Tradition *sells fireplace accessories, baskets, castings, ceramic surrounds, hearths, mantels, and electric, gas, and wood-burning fireplaces.*
17 Passmore Crescent
Brantford, ON
Canada N3T 5L6
Phone: 519-770-0063
www.firesoftradition.com

Heat-N-Glo *manufactures a wide range of gas and wood-burning fireplaces, log sets, and fireplace inserts.*
20802 Kensington Blvd.
Lakeville, MN 55044
Phone: 888-743-2887
Fax: 800-259-1549
www.heatnglo.com

The Hearth, Patio, and Barbecue Association (HPBA) *was established to promote the hearth products industry in North America. Members include distributors, manufacturers, non-profit organizations, associates, retailers, and service companies.*
1601 N. Kent St., Suite 1001
Arlington, VA 22209
Phone: 703-522-0086
Fax: 703-522-0548
http://hpba.org

Hearthlink Outdoor Fireplaces *is a source for cast-aluminum chimineas and fireplaces.*
9 Maple St.
Randolph, VT 05060
Phone: 877-337-8414
Fax: 802-728-4809
www.outdoorfireplaces.com

Heatilator Products *offers a broad line of gas, electric, and wood-burning fireplaces, as well as fireplace inserts, gas logs, and outdoor fireplace products.*
1915 W. Saunders
Mt. Pleasant, IA 52641
Phone: 800-843-2848
Fax: 800-248-2038
www.heatilator.com

resource guide

J.A. Getz Company *sells mantels in a variety of decorative and architectural styles.*
8616 S. 228th St.
Kent, WA 98031
Phone: 253-850-0466
Fax: 253-850-0469
www.jagetz.com

Lennox Hearth Products *makes fireplaces, stoves, inserts, and gas logs.*
1110 W. Taft Ave.
Orange, CA 92865-4150
www.lennoxhearthproducts.com

Majestic Vermont Castings Stoves
manufactures indoor and outdoor gas and wood-burning fireplaces, freestanding stoves, and accessories.
www.majesticgaslogs.com
www.vermontcastings.com

Mantels of Yesteryear *manufactures and sells to the consumer reproduction fireplace mantels in many styles. Delivery is nationwide.*
P.O. Box 908
McCaysville, GA 30555
Phone: 706-492-5534
Fax: 706-492-3758
www.mantelsofyesteryear.com

Martin Gas Products *manufactures fireplaces, fireplace inserts, and gas heaters with different venting options. The company also sells related hearth products. The Web site provides a dealer locator. Martin Gas Products is a division of Martin Gas Industries, Inc.*
Martin Gas Industries, Inc.
301 E. Tennessee St.
Florence, AL 35630
Phone: 866-244-0750
Fax: 256-740-5192
www.martingas.com

Miles Industries/ Valor *sells natural gas fireplaces and fireplace inserts that match classic firebox dimensions. The Web site provides dealer information and an online Btu calculator for determining Btu requirements.*
829 W. Third St.
N. Vancouver, BC
Canada V7P 3K7
Phone: 800-468-2567
Fax: 604-984-0246
www.valorflame.com

Mountain Stream Forge *makes hand-forged, iron fireplace accessories and equipment.*
P.O. Box 262
Canby, OR 97013
Phone: 800-392-4604
Fax: 503-263-6329
www.mountainstreamforge.com

National Chimney Sweep Guild *provides local chimney sweep referrals nationwide.*
2155 Commercial Dr.
Plainfield, IN 46168
Phone: 317-837-1500
Fax: 317-837-5365
www.ncsg.org

Raytech, Inc., *offers an array of fireplace products, including tools, patio heaters, mantels, and wood stoves.*
2 Fallbrook
Irvine, CA 92604
Phone: 800-838-5898
Fax: 949-653-1030
www.raytechstore.com

resource guide

Regency Fireplace Products *manufactures gas-fueled and wood-burning fireplaces and stoves, as well as fireplace inserts. The Regency Web site allows the customer to create and design a personal fireplace look, and to find the nearest dealer.*
www.regencyshowcase.com

Superior Fireplaces *manufactures fireplaces. Superior is affiliated with Lennox Hearth Products. The Web site provides a list of dealers.*
1110 W. Taft Ave.
Orange, CA 92865
www.lennoxhearthproducts.com

Temco Fireplace Products *manufactures gas and wood-burning fireplace products. The Web site provides a list of distributors.*
1190 W. Oleander
Perris, CA 92571
Phone: 909-657-7311
Fax: 909-943-1841
www.temcofireplaces.com

Tulikivi U.S. Inc. *manufactures stoves, cookstoves, and fireplaces.*
One Penn Plaza, Suite 3600
New York, NY 10119
Phone: 212-896-3897
Fax: 212-760-1088
www.tulikivi.com

UniFlame Corporation *specializes in outdoor patio heaters, fireplace accessories, and barbecue grills.*
1817 N. Kenosha Rd.
Zion, IL 60099
Phone: 800-762-1142
Fax: 847-731-6032
www.uniflame.com

Waterford Irish Stoves *makes porcelain enamel, cast-iron wood-burning stoves and wood-burning and gas fireplaces. The Web site offers tips for heating with gas and wood, answers questions related to hearth products, and contains a listing of dealers.*
www.waterfordstoves.com

glossary

Adobe fireplace: A fireplace representative of American Southwest architecture, made of sun-dried brick and generally found in hot climates.

Andiron: A metal-crafted log support with a decorative vertical shaft. It is attached to a horizontal bar mounted on short legs.

Art Deco: A design movement that started in France and became popular in the United States during the 1920s and 1930s. It is characterized by geometric forms, zigzags, inlays, and lacquer finishes.

Art Nouveau: A late-nineteenth-century style that rejects historical references and uses organic forms and sinuous stylized curves as decoration.

Arts and Crafts: A design movement led by architect William Morris in England during the late nineteenth century. It rejected industrialization and encouraged the use of natural materials and hand-craftsmanship. It soon gained popularity in the United States, where it is also called Craftsman style.

Ash dump: An enclosed system that allows for clearing ash from the hearth and emptying it into an ash pit, which is located beneath the firebox.

Asymmetry: The balance between objects of different sizes as the result of placement or grouping.

Balance: The equilibrium among forms in a room or on a surface. Balanced relationships between objects can be either symmetrical or asymmetrical.

Baroque: An exaggerated, heavily ornamented, theatrical seventeenth-century European decorative style that features oversized curves, twisted columns, broken pediments, and large-scale moldings.

Btu: The abbreviation for British thermal unit; a standard measurement of heat energy.

Cape Cod lighter: A small metal pot with a pumice ball on a metal wand. It's used with kerosene as a fire-starter.

Catalytic combustor: A ceramic device that lowers the temperature at which smoke will ignite and burn. A chute directs smoke to a combustion chamber where the combustor burns off particulates.

Ceramic firebox: A firebox engineered of modern refractory materials that makes a fire burn cleaner, hotter, and more efficiently.

Chiminea: An outdoor fire device that originated in seventeenth-century Mexico as a clay oven for baking bread. Today, both traditional clay as well as sturdy metal chimineas are available.

Chimney: The part of the fireplace that transports smoke and other byproducts of the burning fire upward through the roof and into the atmosphere.

Damper: A movable device resembling a plate that spans the lower end of the smoke chamber and opens or closes the fireplace flue.

Damper hanger: A device that hooks onto the end of the damper to show that the damper is closed.

Damper plaque: A small plaque that flips up or down to indicate when the fireplace damper is open or closed, respectively.

Fatwood: Wood cut from pine stumps containing a high amount of flammable resin, sold as a fire-starter.

Federal: Early nineteenth-century American decorative and architectural style, closely resembling that of the English Georgian period. Highly symmetrical, it features classical and patriotic motifs.

Fireback: A vertical metal accessory placed behind the fire to absorb heat and radiate it back into the room.

Fireboard: A decorative covering that can be placed in front of the opening when the fireplace is not in use.

Firebox: The part of the fireplace that contains the burning fuel and fire. It is also referred to as the fire chamber.

Fire pit: A wood-, gas-, or alcohol gel-fueled device used for outdoor fires. It can be made of metal (portable) or custom-built using masonry (permanent).

Fire-starter logs: A treated rectangular block of sawdust and wax used to start a fire.

Flue: The passageway that transports the byproducts of burning fuel to the outside atmosphere.

Georgian: A predominently eighteenth-century English architecture and furniture style that is elegant, symmetrical, and classical in form. It was inspired by the excavations of ancient sites in Greece and Pompeii.

Harmony: The coherence of different design elements achieved by color, shape, or motif.

Hearth: The floor of the firebox. It sometimes extends past the fireplace into the room.

Hearth rug: A protection for the floor made of wool, which is naturally fire-resistant, or synthetic materials treated with flame-retardant chemicals.

Line: In design terms, line defines space. Different lines (vertical, horizontal, diagonal, curved) denote various qualities.

Lintel: The horizontal support spanning the top opening at the front of the firebox.

Mantel: The shelf that is mounted above the fireplace opening and across the face.

Noncatalytic stove: A stove built with a second chamber outside the firebox where smoke is directed.

Patio heater: An outdoor heating source usually consisting of a heater within a dome. Most patio heaters provide heat within a 15- to 20-foot radius.

Proportion: The relationship of parts or objects to one another based on size.

Rhythm: In design terms, moving the eye around a room at a measured pace set up by repeating motifs, colors, or shapes.

Rococo: Predominently French and German eighteenth-century decorative movement that reacted to classicism. It features elaborately carved naturalistic forms such as flora and fauna.

Scale: The size of something as it relates to the size of everything else around it.

Smoke chamber: The area between the damper and the opening of the flue.

Smoke shelf: The floor at the back of the smoke chamber.

Surround: The facing ornamentation on the sides and top of the fireplace opening.

Symmetry: The identical arrangement of objects, forms, or parts on both sides of a centerline.

Throat: The narrow opening aiding the flow of smoke, gas, and flames into the smoke chamber and out through the chimney.

index

index

photo credits

page 1: Alise O'Brien page 2: Alise O'Brien, designer: Kim Plunkett page 5: Mark Samu, faux finish artist: Lu Samu page 6: Mark Lohman, designer: Lynn Pries page 7: *top to bottom* Tria Giovan; Tim Street-Porter/ Beate Works, designer: Jeffrey Weisman; Mark Lohman, designer: Debra Jones; Tria Giovan page 9: Brian Vanden Brink, architect: Mark Hutker & Associates page 10: Mark Lohman, designer: Lynn Pries page 11: *top* Mark Lohman, designer: William Hefner; *bottom* Tony Giammarino page 13: Jessie Walker, designer: Paul Lauren Designs page 14: Brian Vanden Brink, builder: James Beyor page 15: Tim-Street Porter/ Beate Works, designer: Annie Kelly page 16: Nancy Hill, designer: Diana Sawicki Interior Design page 17: Tim Street-Porter/ Beate Works, designer: Corrigan page 18: Brian Vanden Brink page 19: Brian Vanden Brink page 20: Brian Vanden Brink, Heartwood Log Homes pages 22-23: all photos by Tim Street-Porter/ Beate Works, designer, *top middle:* Jeffrey Weisman; architect, *top right:* Brian Murphy; designer, *bottom right:* Mark Mack; architect, *bottom middle left:* Brian Murphy; designer, *bottom left:* Christin Hubert page 24: Mark Lohman, designer: Janet Lohman page 26: *top* Beth Singer; *bottom* Mark Lohman page 27: Mark Lohman, designer: Kitty Bartholomew page 28: Mark Lohman, designer: Christine Hallen-Burg page 29: *top* Tony Giammarino; *bottom* Tim Street-Porter/ Beate Works (photographed at Casa Del Herraro), architect: George Washington Smith page 30: Nancy Hill, designer: Deborah T. Lipner, LTD Interiors page 31: *top* Mark Lohman, designer: Lynn Pries; *bottom* Mark Lohman, designer: Kathryne Designs page 32: Tim Street-Porter/ Beate Works, artist: Nancy Kintisch page 33: Mark Lohman, designer: Debra Jones page 34: *top and bottom* Beth Singer page 35: *bottom* Mark Samu, faux finish artist: Lu Samu pages 36-37: *top left* Brian Vanden Brink, architects: Scogin Elam and Bray; *top middle* Mark Samu; *top right & bottom right* Bob Greenspan Photography, stylist: Sue Andrews; *bottom middle* Brian Vanden Brink; *bottom left* Tim Street-Porter/ Beate Works, architects: Greene and Greene pages 38-39: Mark Lohman page 40: Philip Clayton-Thompson Photography page 41: *top* Mark Lohman, designer: Douglas Burdge; *bottom* Tria Giovan page 42: *top* Mark Samu page 43: *top* Jessie Walker; *bottom* Mark Lohman page 44: Jessie Walker, designer: Carol Knott page 45: Mark Lohman, designer: William Hefner page 46: *top* Mark Samu; *bottom* Tria Giovan page 47: Mark Samu, designer: Rinaldi Associates page 48: Mark Lohman page 49: *top* Tria Giovan; *bottom* Mark Lohman, designer: Janet Lohman page 50: *top* Jessie Walker, designer: Kim Elia; *bottom* Mark Lohman, designer: Dan Marty page 51: Tria Giovan page 52: *top* Tria Giovan page 53: *top & bottom* Tria Giovan pages 54-55: *top left* Tria Giovan; *top middle* Jessie Walker; *top right* Brian Vanden Brink; *bottom right* Brian Vanden Brink, architect: Thom Rouselle; *bottom middle right* davidduncanlivingston.com; *bottom middle left* Mark Lohman, designer: Jim Baker; *bottom left* Mark Lohman page 56: Brian Vanden Brink page 58: davidduncanlivingston.com page 59: Tim Street-Porter/ Beate Works page 60: Tim Street-Porter/ Beate Works, architect: Frank Gehry page 61: Mark Lohman, designer: Harry Topping page 62:

Brian Vanden Brink page 63: Brian Vanden Brink, architect: John Morris page 64: Tim Street-Porter/ Beate Works page 65: Randall Perry page 67: Brian Vanden Brink pages 68-69: *top left* courtesy of Aladdin Steel Products; *top middle* davidduncanlivingston.com; *top right* Randall Perry; *bottom right* Randall Perry; *bottom middle* courtesy of Heat-n-Glo; *bottom left* Brian Vanden Brink pages 70-71: Beth Singer page 72: *top* Mark Samu; *bottom* courtesy of Fire Designs page 73: Mark Lohman, designer: Christine Hallen-Burg page 74: *top* courtesy of Hearthlink Outdoor Fireplaces; *bottom* Tony Giammarino page 75: *top* courtesy of Hearthlink Outdoor Fireplaces page 76: Tim Street-Porter/ Beate Works, designer: Jon Jerde page 77: Tim Street-Porter/ Beate Works, architect: Jose de Yturbe page 78: *top* courtesy of California Redwood Association; *bottom* courtesy of Fire Designs page 79: courtesy of California Redwood Association page 80: Tim Street-Porter/ Beate Works page 81: courtesy of Endless Summer Patio Heaters/ Uniflame page 82: *top left* courtesy of Heat-n-Glo; *top right* courtesy of Hearthlink Outdoor Fireplaces; *bottom* Tria Giovan page 83: *top left* Bob Greenspan Photography, stylist: Sue Andrews; *top right* Mark Lohman; *bottom left* Melabee M Miller; *bottom right* courtesy of Fire Designs page 84: Jessie Walker page 86: Brian Vanden Brink page 87: *top* courtesy of Heatilator, Inc.; *bottom* Mark Samu page 88: *top* Jessie Walker; *bottom* Bill Rothschild page 89: Jessie Walker page 90: courtesy of Aladdin Steel Products page 91: Brian Vanden Brink, architects: Elliot & Elliot page 92: *top* Jessie Walker; *bottom right* Jessie Walker; *bottom left* courtesy of Heatilator, Inc. page 93: *top left* Jessie Walker; *top right* courtesy of Heatilator, Inc.; *bottom* Brian Vanden Brink, architect: Sam Van Dam pages 94-95: Brad Simmons, stylist: Joetta Moulden page 96: *top* Tim Street-Porter/ Beate Works, designer: Barbara Barry; *bottom* Tria Giovan page 97: Mark Samu page 98: Tria Giovan page 99: Brian Vanden Brink, architect: Turner Brooks page 100: *top* Mark Lohman, designer: Sheldon Harte; *bottom* Brian Vanden Brink, architect: Elliot & Elliot page 101: davidduncanlivingston.com page 102: *top* Mark Samu, designer: Eileen Boyd Designs; *bottom* Mark Samu, stylist: Tia Burns page 103: Brian Vanden Brink, designer: Mark Hutger page 104: *top and bottom* Tria Giovan page 105: George Ross page 106: *top* Brad Simmons, stylist: Joetta Moulden; *bottom* Brian Vanden Brink, architect: Design Group Three, designer: Christina Oliver page 107: Mark Lohman, designer: Douglas Burdge page 108: *top left* Mark Samu; *top right* Mark Samu; *bottom right* Mark Samu; *bottom left* Tim Street-Porter/ Beate Works page 109: *top left* Mark Samu; *top right* Mark Lohman; *bottom right* Mark Samu page 111: Tim Street-Porter/ Beate Works, architect: Brian Murphy page 112: Lisa Masson page 115: Randall Perry page 116: Robert Perron page 119: Carolyn Bates, architect: Evan Lipencott page 120: Karen Melvin, designer: Gep Durenberger page 121: Anne Gummerson, designer: R. Walker, LLC page 122: Tim Street-Porter/ Beate Works, architect: Scott Johnson page 125: Karen Melvin, designer: Eric Oder, A.I.A., mural design: Sara Susanka, A.I.A., faux painter: Maureen Lyttle page 126: Melabee M Miller

Have a decorating, home improvement, or gardening project? Look for these and other fine **Creative Homeowner books** at your local home center or bookstore.

Portfolio of 250+ ispirational color photos, plus design and planning tips. 128 pp.; 8½"×10⅞"
BOOK #: 277155

Design inspiration for gaining functional space. Over 200 color photographs. 144 pp.; 8½"×10⅞"
BOOK #: 279430

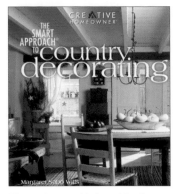

Fill your home with the spirit of country: fabrics, finishes, and furniture. 200+ photos. 176 pp.; 9"×10"
BOOK #: 279685

How to work with space, color, pattern, and texture. Over 400 color photos. 288 pp.; 9"×10"
BOOK #: 279672

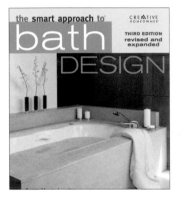

All you need to know about designing a bathroom. Over 275 color photos. 224 pp.; 9¼"×10⅞"
BOOK #: 279239

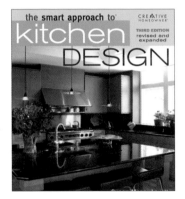

How to create kitchen style like a pro. Over 275 color photographs. 224 pp.; 9¼"×10⅞"
BOOK #: 279952

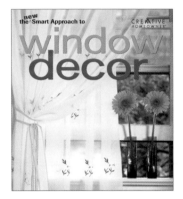

Choose a window treatment like a professional designer. 250 color photos. 208 pp.; 9"×10"
BOOK #: 279438

Create a beautiful and safe environment for your baby. 260+ color photos. 208 pp.; 9"×10"
BOOK #: 279482

An impressive guide to garden design and plant selection. 950+ color photos. 384 pp.; 9"×10"
BOOK #: 274610

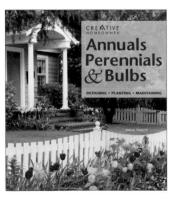

Lavishly illustrated with portraits of over 100 flowering plants. 500+ color photos. 208 pp.; 9"×10"
BOOK #: 274032

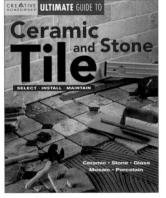

Everything you need to know about setting ceramic tile. Over 500 photos. 224 pp.; 8½"×10⅞"
BOOK #: 277532

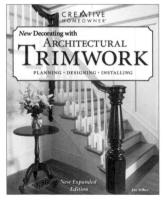

Transform a room with trimwork. Over 550 color photos and illustrations. 240 pp.; 8½"×10⅞"
BOOK #: 277500